Beyond Methodology

NEW DIRECTIONS IN LANGUAGE TEACHING
Editors: Howard B. Altman and Peter Strevens

This important series is for language teachers and others who:
– need to be informed about the key issues facing the language teaching
  profession today;
– want to understand the theoretical issues underlying current debates;
– wish to relate theory to classroom practice.

In this series:

Beyond Methodology

Second Language Teaching and the Community

Mary Ashworth

The right of the
University of Cambridge
to print and sell
all manner of books
was granted by
Henry VIII in 1534.
The University has printed
and published continuously
since 1584.

Cambridge University Press
Cambridge
New York   Port Chester
Melbourne   Sydney

Published by the Press Syndicate of the University of Cambridge
The Pitt Building, Trumpington Street, Cambridge CB2 1RP
40 West 20th Street, New York, NY 10011–4211, USA
10 Stamford Road, Oakleigh, Victoria 3166, Australia

First published 1985
Third printing 1992

Printed in Malta
by Interprint Ltd

Library of Congress cataloguing in publication data

Ashworth Mary.

Beyond methodology.

(New directions in language teaching)

Bibliography: p.
Includes index.
1. Language and languages – Study and teaching – Social aspects.
2. Language planning. 3. English language – Study and teaching.
I. Title. II. Series
P53.8.A7   1985   418'.007   85-11024

British Library cataloguing in publication data

Ashworth, Mary

Beyond methodology: second language teaching and the
community – (New directions in language teaching)
1. English language – Study and teaching – Foreign speakers
I. Title   II. Series
428.2'4'07   PE1128.A2

ISBN 0 521 26665 3 hardback
ISBN 0 521 31991 9 paperback

UP

Contents

Contents

5 Teaching English internationally

6 Predicting the future in language teaching

To Jean Handscombe and Strini Reddy
for their untiring work on behalf of immigrant
and native children.

Acknowledgements

I would like to acknowledge with gratitude the advice and support I have received in the preparation of this book from H. Patricia Wakefield and Lee Gunderson of the Language Education Department, Faculty of Education, University of British Columbia; Howard Altman and Peter Strevens, the series editors; and Peter Donovan of Cambridge University Press.

Introduction

In recent years education has had a somewhat uneasy relationship with the communities it serves. Perhaps part of the problem has been that neither side has listened with sufficient care, patience and understanding to what the other side has been saying. Or perhaps the problem has been that neither side has been articulating its concerns thoughtfully and clearly. Teachers, who often comment that they are happiest when they are working with students in the intimacy of their classrooms, have tended to be far too quiet about what they have achieved during these years of tremendous social, political and economic flux and what the problems are which they and their students face day after day.

During the past decade, the education of children and adults has been subjected not only to criticism but also to attempts by various pressure groups to change current practices. Along with other disciplines, second language teaching has come under attack. If the profession is to respond in a responsible fashion in words or actions, it must be aware of both its shortcomings and its achievements. When it is apparent that change is needed, teachers and administrators should, because of their knowledge and experience, be a part of the change-making process and not simply the passive recipients of other people's policies. But language teachers sometimes hesitate to get involved with the various communities which benefit from their work, supply their resources, and exercise some control over their activities. Perhaps they have met with rebuff. Perhaps they view involvement as a political action and want no part of it. But whatever the reasons, the fact is that the establishment of good second language programs and of good teaching/learning conditions cannot occur without the quiet, sustained efforts of caring and knowledgeable teachers working in and with communities that lie beyond the classroom – beyond methodology..

The purpose of this book is to delineate more clearly what some of the relationships are between second language teachers and the various communities which they serve and which serve them, and to suggest ways in which teachers and communities – local, national, and international – can work more closely for the benefit of both individual students and society as a whole.

The first three chapters will therefore begin by examining the three roles that communities play vis-à-vis second language teaching: the community as beneficiary, the community as resource, and the community as control. Each of these chapters will raise issues and suggest some positive and practical actions. Chapter 4 will consider how national policies affect second language teachers and how teachers might, in turn, affect policy-making and implementation. Chapter 5 looks at teaching English internationally. Finally, chapter 6 suggests ways in which language teachers can, by trying to predict the future, exercise a modicum of control over it.

This book is directed towards practicing second language teachers and teachers-in-training, to consultants, supervisors and administrators of language programs, and to members of the public who are interested in some aspect of second language teaching, whether ESL (English as a Second Language), EFL (English as a Foreign Language), modern or foreign language teaching, heritage or vernacular language teaching, or bilingual education. However, as no two language programs are identical, that is, they do not occur in identical situations in identical communities, readers must take the ideas presented in this book and consider their relevance to their own situations. In other words, readers must follow the old adage of *adopting* those ideas that might work for them, *adapting* them to their particular situations, and *improving* them.

1 The community as beneficiary

This chapter will examine major issues in language planning and the language-planning process. It will outline ways in which individuals and communities benefit from the work of language teachers.

1.1 Overview

Is second language teaching a worthwhile profession? Would it make any difference to the lives of millions of children and adults in language classrooms all over the world if there were no language teachers? Michael Long writes '...a review of research findings concludes that there is considerable (although not overwhelming) evidence that instruction is beneficial 1) for children as well as adults, 2) for beginning, intermediate, and advanced students, 3) on integrative as well as discrete-point tests, and 4) in acquisition-rich as well as acquisition-poor environments.'[1] But what do researchers measure? Perhaps the acquisition of particular grammatical items, or a change in attitude towards the target language and culture, or the ability to comprehend a reading passage. There are, however, many intangibles in second language teaching which defy measurement. How can we measure the psychological effect on a new immigrant of being able to produce a few words in halting English and to understand the reply? How can we measure the contribution to a developing nation of a native-born technician trained overseas after first learning the new language of instruction in his own country? How can we measure the sense of pride engendered in a small ethnic community whose children live and learn in two languages and two cultures? How can we measure the growing unity and harmony in a nation whose citizens have equal access to economic security regardless of what language they speak at home? The fact is that we cannot. We sense, however, that there are some values inherent in second language teaching which are important enough to cause governments and institutions all over the world to engage in language planning so that young children, adults and senior citizens can have access to second-language-teaching classes. If that were not so, there would be little point in this book or in the thousands of methodology or student texts which have been published over the years.

Language teaching in its various forms benefits society in various ways and to varying degrees. To clarify those benefits the first section (1.2) will provide a brief outline of language planning and the terminology associated with it. The second section (1.3) will examine the major issues that face language planners. The following section (1.4) will consider the language-planning process. The next section (1.5) will describe various language-teaching programs, and the last section (1.6) will draw attention to the benefits of language-teaching programs to individuals, communities and nations.

1.2 Language planning

The concept of language planning is relatively new. It came into prominence with the publication in 1966 of Joshua A. Fishman's book *Language Loyalty in the United States*. Since then language planning has become an increasingly important field of study as people have recognized that language often lies at the heart of some social and political problems.

While in the past language planning was not the science it is today, there were nonetheless good reasons why languages were taught. L. G. Kelly suggests that three aims run like braided threads through the past two thousand years, first one on top and then another:

> In language teaching three broad aims can be distinguished: the social, the artistic (or literary), and the philosophical. The first aim demands that language should be regarded as a form of social behavior and a type of communication. The artistic aim treats language as a vehicle for creativity, demanding both appreciation of creative activity and creative activity itself. This aim is often split into its active and passive aspects. The philosophical aim demands training in analytical techniques and often confuses linguistics with language teaching. At each period in history one of these has become predominant, generating its own approach to method.[2]

For centuries language teaching has been a part of formal education. The trivium of the Middle Ages, which had been handed down from Roman days, consisted of grammar, rhetoric and dialectic. In order to read their great religious texts, Jewish scholars have learned Hebrew and Aramaic, Hindus have mastered Sanskrit, Moslems have studied classical Arabic, and Christians have struggled with Greek and Latin. In the past, language teachers have tried to develop skills in their students so that they could achieve fame as orators, or administer multilingual empires, or create literary masterpieces, or act as international entrepreneurs. More recently language teachers have been concerned that their students can have access to higher education, or maintain their ethnic identity, or integrate into a new society. Today, the speed with which mankind communicates electronically coupled with the growing tension in and between local, national and international communities makes it imperative that language planning be carried out so that people around the world can talk, not fight. However, before getting deeper into the topic, readers may find it helpful to become familiar with some of the terms used in this and other books that relate to language planning.

In 1951, a special committee of Unesco met in Paris to consider the use of vernacular languages. During its discussions, in order to avoid misunderstanding or ambiguity, the committee produced the following definitions of language types, still used and quoted today:

Indigenous language: The language of the people considered to be the original inhabitants of an area.

Lingua franca: A language which is used habitually by people whose mother tongues are different in order to facilitate communication between them.

Mother or native tongue: The language which a person acquires in early years and which normally becomes his natural instrument of thought and communication.

National language: The language of a political, social and cultural entity.

Official language: A language used in the business of government – legislative, executive and judicial.

Pidgin: A language which has arisen as the result of contact between peoples of different language, usually formed from a mixing of the languages.

Regional language: A language which is used as a medium of communication between peoples living within a certain area who have different mother tongues.

Second language: A language acquired by a person in addition to his mother tongue.

Vernacular language: A language which is the mother tongue of a group which is socially or politically dominated by another group speaking a different language.

World language: A language used over wide areas of the world.[3]

A few years later, W. A. Stewart suggested some additional categories defined according to the functions of language in society, summarized here as follows:

Capital language: A language used as the primary medium of communication in the vicinity of the national capital. This function is particularly important in countries where political power, social prestige, and economic activity are centred in the capital.

Group language: A language used as the normal medium of communication among the members of a single cultural or ethnic group, such as a tribe, settled group of immigrants, etc. (Note: in this book the terms 'heritage' or 'ancestral' language will be used instead of 'group' language as they bring out the sense of history, often so important to minorities.)

Educational language: A language used as a medium of primary or secondary education, either regionally or nationally.

School subject language: A language commonly taught as a subject in secondary and/or higher education.

Literary language: A language used primarily for literary or scholarly purposes.

Religious language: A language used primarily in connection with the ritual of a particular religion.[4]

1.3   Major issues in language planning

Because language permeates every sector of our social, political, educational, and economic life, language issues can be found everywhere. Hence, no society can carry on its day-to-day existence without language policies; however, these may be implicit rather than explicit. To facilitate discussion, these issues will be presented under the headings of national unity, economic development, education, and linguistic and cultural heritage maintenance.

National unity

Linguistic nationalism has become an important symbol of a people's political identity. It has been, and is likely to remain, a powerful and therefore a potentially unifying or divisive force. In the past, countries which were virtually unilingual were spared the often hostile debates which surrounded the choice of an official language in bilingual or multilingual countries; however, the mass migrations of people across the globe that have occurred during this century have forced former unilingual countries, such as Great Britain, to face the reality of linguistic diversity. Meanwhile, long-established bilingual countries such as Belgium and Canada are still arguing internally over language rights for their two official language groups. Elsewhere the emerging multilingual nations of Africa and Asia have been trying to choose from a number of languages – local, regional or world-wide – one or more languages that will foster national unity by helping the users to feel that they are a political entity. Good order, a necessary adjunct to national unity, depends upon a government's ability to provide effective administration through a language or languages acceptable to and understood by the citizens.

For developing nations the choice of an official language often poses problems. Many of the newly independent countries of Africa were created during the last century by European nations who paid little attention to speech boundaries. Some speech communities were cut in two, while elsewhere tribes traditionally hostile to each other were forced to come together under an alien administration which imposed its language upon the people. Independence required these unnatural geo-political communities to adopt at least one official language for administration and education. But which language(s)? New nations faced one or more of the following problems:

1. due to old traditional rivalries, no native language was acceptable to all speech communities; or
2. at the time of independence, none of the local vernaculars was sufficiently developed in the language of science or technology to permit its immediate use in post-secondary education or in the modernization or industrialization of the economy; or
3. attitudes towards the departing colonizing power were sufficiently hostile as to make the continued use of its language unacceptable.

In Uganda, English was chosen as the official language, but other languages were given official regional status. In Tanzania, Swahili, an African language which had spread from its southern home to more northern areas, became the official language even though it was not spoken as a first language by all of the citizens. As English, however, is used in post-secondary education in Tanzania, membership in certain circles depends on a knowledge of both languages in addition to the local vernacular. Kenya made no pronouncement regarding which language(s) were to be considered official, but permitted both English and Swahili to be used in government and parliament. To have declared any one language as the official language would have been to invite strong reactions from powerful tribal groups. If conflicting language loyalties had been given an opportunity for expression in the early years of independence, national unity might have been impossible.

When language is associated with religion, trouble can arise. In the huge sub-continent of India, particularly in the north where Urdu-speaking Moslems, Hindi-speaking Hindus, and Punjabi-speaking Sikhs live side-by-side, independence brought violence and bloodshed as Moslems battled Hindus for the right to self-determination in their own Islamic nation of Pakistan. Today, some Sikhs are hoping that they too will separate from India and set up a third nation founded on language and religion.

In 1957 Malaysia gained its independence from Britain. It inherited four separate school systems each using a different language as the medium of instruction. The most prestigious was the English-medium system from which graduates could enter universities in Malaysia,

Singapore, or elsewhere in the British Commonwealth. The least prestigious was the Malay-medium system which provided only six years of primary education following which the majority of the students were expected to return to the land. The other two systems used either Chinese (Mandarin) or Tamil. The new Malaysian government immediately made Malay the national language, and declared that by 1967 it would be the sole official language and hence the medium of instruction in all government or government-assisted schools. The ten-year transition period was to be used to standardize the spelling, prepare textbooks, and train teachers. Schools began to phase in Malay while continuing to teach English, which was considered to be an important component in modernizing the country through science and technology. But the imposition of Malay on businesses and schools resulted in race riots in the 1960s so that in 1971 the Sedition Act was passed which prohibited people from engaging in public discussion on sensitive issues such as citizenship or the national language policy. While, in fact, it took almost twenty-six years for the schools to fully implement Malay as the medium of instruction, a faster rate might have caused more problems than it solved by failing to give people adequate time to adjust. National unity is not achieved over night. The fusion of a number of ethnic groups into a cohesive national group takes years, during which time hostility and bitterness can grow if the soil is fertile. Meanwhile, the emerging nation must continue to develop politically, economically, educationally and socially as best it can.

Problems within the developed nations are of a different order. Tradition may have established one language as the official language, and tradition is often hard to break even in the face of common sense or common justice in changing times. In the southwestern United States, Spanish, which is widely used, is not recognized as an official language. Indeed, some people fear that bilingual education will produce even larger pockets of Spanish-speaking Americans which might result in the linguistic balkanization of the United States, and they would like to see English enshrined in the Constitution as the only official language. Others question how such a move is congruent with the notion of cultural pluralism.

Attitudes projected towards languages tend to reflect attitudes towards people; that is, the admiration, hostility or ambivalence shown to a language may reflect the attitudes projected towards the speakers of that language. Consequently the imposition of bilingualism upon monolingual people who live in a country where two languages are spoken in two relatively distinct regions may well be resented. Canada is a case in point. Since 1759 when the French government gave up its territorial claim to Canada, French and English Canadians have existed side-by-side. While English Canadians spread across Canada becoming the dominant group in all provinces but Quebec, French Canadians built their homeland in 'La Belle Province' with pockets of francophones in the Maritimes and Manitoba. But it has not been a harmonious coexistence; antagonism and suspicion on both sides coupled with a lack of genuine cooperation have left Canadians today wondering whether the nation can survive as a federation of provinces which recognize the French and English languages and cultures as of equal value, or whether it must inevitably split into two nations, one French-speaking and one English-speaking. The defeat of the referendum in Quebec in 1980 on 'sovereignty association' did not close the matter. Complicating the situation further are the recently articulated desires of the native people and some of the other minority groups to use their languages in some situations where formerly only French or English were permitted, such as education, or, in the case of the native people, in self-government. The language issue in Canada is still highly emotional and can become a minefield of disaster for the unwary politician who does not tread lightly.

The last century has witnessed mass migrations of people, voluntary and involuntary, from one part of the world to another. Many of the receiving countries are fairly well-developed economically and can, in time, absorb the immigrants into the workforce except in periods of unemployment when resentment quickly builds against the newcomers. Over the years, however, pockets of ethnic minorities establish themselves and, to varying degrees, try to maintain their ancestral language and some of its associated culture. This action may be resented by members of the dominant group who see these ethnic ghettos as intrusions into their established sense of national unity and cohesion, and riots, such as those experienced in Britain in 1982, occur. Pressure is put on governments to promote assimilation through programs which teach the official language and through policies which limit the use of the heritage language. While any nation which accepts speakers of other languages as potential citizens has a responsibility to ensure that the newcomers learn enough of the official language to enable them to participate in the political, social, vocational and educational life of the nation and to contribute to it, this can be done without undermining the first language. But the decision to supplement and not supplant may cause friction in a nation where the bulk of the people believe in total assimilation and are not prepared to consider any alternative.

Language planning will make little headway in any country unless it is sanctioned and promoted by the government which must seek to answer two questions: 1) Which language or languages shall be designated official regional or national languages? The choice of language may affect the relative status of speakers of different languages, raising the status of those who speak the chosen language and lowering the status of those who speak the rejected language. If the language chosen is not an international language, considerable work may have to be done on modernizing the vocabulary and printing textbooks. The choice of the official language can therefore have wide social, political, economic and educational ramifications. 2) Who shall have access to programs teaching the official language or teaching in the official language? When a certain stratum of society is denied the right to learn the official language, it is also denied the right of entry to the power structure. This results in a two-tiered society based on language proficiency, a situation not conducive to national unity over the long run. For many countries a peaceful future seems to lie in the ability of their citizens to find room within their boundaries for people of diverse languages and cultures while pursuing common human goals relating to the quality of life.

Economic development

It is possible for education, and hence language teaching, to make a significant contribution to the economic development of a country if it assists that country in reaching some of its economic goals, which might be

– to raise the standard of living through industrialization and/or modernization;
– to give the citizens greater economic security throughout their lives;
– to produce the goods and services the consumers need;
– to increase exports;
– to be more self-sufficient.

By investing in human capital through a sound basic education along with vocational and retraining programs, governments help to build an informed workforce of skilled technicians and managers. The net effect can be greater efficiency resulting in increased productivity and a rise in the gross national product. In addition, the earning power of individuals is affected by their levels of education and productivity, which in turn affects their spending power. Governments can over-invest in one form of human capital – say, professionals such as doctors, lawyers, and engineers – and under-invest in technicians or semi-skilled workers. When an economy is expanding and there are insufficient technicians or tradesmen to satisfy the demand, migrant workers may be brought in who may need to learn the language of the workplace – though not always. For example, in some English-speaking countries the language used in a factory may be that of the employer, himself an immigrant, who hires his labor from his own ethnic group. But in other factories, where English is the language of communication, skilled immigrant workers may be put to low-level tasks because they cannot take instructions in English.

During the last thirty years, many previously underdeveloped countries have sought to industrialize and modernize their economies by bringing in foreign experts or by sending their young people overseas to study the theory and practice of today's technology and science. The teaching of foreign languages has been central to the success of many of the programs. One outstanding example is that of the People's Republic of China where, in order to achieve its goals of the four modernizations – industry, agriculture, science and technology, and national defence – the state has looked to the west for help. Administrators, teachers, technicans, business people, foresters, agriculturalists and others have been sent abroad to study so that, on their return, they can apply whatever is suitable and relevant to the situation in China. To achieve this end, programs to teach languages of wider communication have been mounted within China and native speakers of those languages have been in demand as instructors.

The fierce competition in international trade markets has seen an increase in foreign language programs designed specifically for business people. Some Japanese firms which deal with English-speaking countries now employ their own instructors of English as a foreign language. Entrepreneurs and salesmen must not only understand the language of the marketplace, they must be familiar with the culture, and they must understand what strategies will win or lose business in the foreign market. Various careers are now opening up for people trained in business and speaking more than one language: technical translators of business letters and manuals; interpreters; overseas salesmen; bilingual secretaries and receptionists; consultants; advertising copywriters; and tour guides.

As nations expand the list of their trading partners, the number of target languages increases. The rise of Japan, Taiwan, Korea and China as industrial powers has forced an interest in their languages in foreign business communities, while within those nations a knowledge of modern languages is seen as desirable. Perhaps in time a wider range of foreign-language options will be available in schools throughout the world as educators recognize the role of language teaching in the economic growth of the community, and as forward-looking administrators and economists plan together to develop this societal resource of language.

Education

Questions regarding language issues in education fall into two categories: political and pedagogical. Political questions deal with which languages will be officially sanctioned to be used and taught in educational institutions and who will have access to language-teaching programs;

that is, the well-being of the state is paramount. Pedagogical questions deal with the best way to educate students from various language backgrounds; that is, the well-being of the student is paramount. Let us suppose, for example, that it is policy in a multilingual nation to have only one official language. Is it compatible with that policy to permit children to be taught through the medium of another language? (Political question.) On the other hand, if children make better progress when they are taught, at least initially, in their mother tongue, should they not be taught in that language? (Pedagogical question.) The major issues facing language planners in education are 1) which language or languages shall be used as the medium of instruction? 2) which language or languages shall be taught as subjects? 3) who will have access to language-teaching programs?

According to William Mackey, in bilingual and multilingual areas four options are open to the planner in choosing the medium of instruction.

1. *Nationality*. The child must take his schooling in the language of the country, regardless of his ethnic origin, religious affiliation, or of the language which he speaks at home, for example, much of the United States.
2. *Territoriality*. The child gets his schooling in the language of the community in which he happens to be living, for example, Switzerland.
3. *Religious affiliation*. This may apply in countries where linguistic divisions coincide to a great extent with religious ones, for example, the province of Quebec in Canada.
4. *Ethnic origin*. Where bilingual communities are closely intermingled the policy may be to have the child do his schooling in the language which he normally speaks at home, for example, parts of South Africa.[5]

Where the school is seen as a political instrument with the responsibility to assimilate all children into one cultural and linguistic mould, then only one language will be permitted as the medium of instruction, that of the dominant group. To allow any other language to be used is to give that language and its associated culture some validity, as languages used or taught in school have higher status than those which are not. A unilingual policy presents no difficulties in unilingual nations, but can cause dissension in communities or nations where two languages exist in reasonably close proximity and where there is a perceived need – social, educational, or economic – either to learn the other language or to maintain one's own. Three possible situations are as follows:

1. Speakers of a minority language may live in an enclave either geographically isolated from speakers of the dominant official lan-

guage or encircled by them and dependent upon them economically. They need to interact with the dominant group while preserving their own identity.

2. Speakers of different languages of equal prestige may live adjacent to each other and may develop a degree of interdependence that could be enhanced by knowing the other language.
3. Migrant workers may settle for short or long periods in countries where their language is not spoken, but it is their intention that they and their children will return to their homeland at some future date and pick up life in the mother tongue.

For these groups a unilingual policy is not sufficient. What are the alternatives? We will look first at alternatives for children, followed by alternatives for adults.

VERNACULAR LANGUAGE TEACHING

In many countries of the world no single language is spoken and understood by all the inhabitants, which results in some children having to take all or part of their education in a second language. Educationally, however, there is evidence to suggest that children taught in their early years in a second language do not do as well as those who begin their schooling in their vernacular. If young children are required to learn new concepts in school in a language which is foreign to them, they will be able neither to grasp the explanations offered, nor to use language to expand and refine those concepts. If thinking skills are delayed while children struggle to learn the second language, their intellectual development will be retarded. As language skills developed in one language can be transferred to another language, vernacular language teaching can assist both cognitive and linguistic development. In addition, struggling to learn at an early age in another group's language does not engender pride in one's own ethnicity, a factor which may contribute to low achievement.

Vernacular language teaching was advocated by Edgar Faure et al. in *Learning To Be* (1972), an official publication of Unesco, who said, 'It is essential that the language spoken in a child's family be used during the first stages of his education.'[6] Vernacular language teaching is sanctioned in Russia, China, and some African countries, and in some parts of the English-speaking world where numbers permit. It usually lasts for about three years during which time the second language, which will be used exclusively in secondary and post-secondary education, is added. However, while the use of the children's own language in their early education would seem to be their right, this may conflict with their right to the best education possible as it has been customary in some parts of the world to use as vernacular language teachers people who have failed to make the grade as teachers capable of using or teaching the official language. A low level of vernacular language teaching may therefore be more damaging to children than competent teaching of and in the second language.

Isaura Santiago outlines the needs and issues most often raised in the literature regarding vernacular language teaching:

1. the need to improve language-planning efforts, to increase vernacular language instruction, to resolve the inadequacies of the vernacular as a medium of instruction, and to develop/obtain effective models for first and second or multilingual language learning;
2. the need to translate curricula and curriculum models;
3. the need for more textbooks, materials, technology, and methodologies in vernacular/bilingual language;
4. the need to include culture in the curriculum, most often seen as a subject (history) or content (social studies) rather than form;
5. the need for teachers who speak vernacular languages and the need to improve their skills.[7]

BILINGUAL EDUCATION

Bilingual education is not new. Over the course of time and in many parts of the world, bilingual education has been the norm rather than the exception. However, as Charles A. Ferguson et al. point out, 'The implicit goals of bilingual education vary from society to society; they often overlap within a given society and may or may not reflect the aims of the society as a whole.'[8] They offer as a starting point the following list of implicit goals for bilingual education:

1. *To assimilate individuals or groups into the mainstream of society.* The aim is to socialize people for full participation in the community.
2. *To unify a multilingual society.* The aim is to bring unity to a multiethnic, multitribal, or multinational linguistically diverse polity.
3. *To enable people to communicate with the outside world.* The aim is to introduce language of wider communication in addition to the unifying national language so as to make it possible for nationals to interact with foreigners.
4. *To gain an economic advantage for individuals or groups.* The aim is to provide language skills which are salable in the job market and can put a person ahead on jobs and status.
5. *To preserve ethnic or religious ties.* The preservation of ethnic or religious identity in an individual or group may or may not go against general national goals.

6. *To reconcile different political, or socially separate, communities.* Language can mediate between social or political groups. The implication may be that the more fortunate have a responsibility to the less fortunate which can be fulfilled partially by learning their language to communicate with them.

7. *To spread and maintain the use of a colonial language.* This goal, which is similar to the mainstream goal, is to socialize an entire population to a colonial existence and a colonial language.

8. *To embellish or strengthen the education of elites.* Much of bilingual education in the world is primarily for elites, and much of that which is now generally available to all began as education for elites.

9. *To give equal status to languages of unequal prominence in the society.* As a democratic or egalitarian policy, two languages of unequal status in a nation may be treated as exactly equal under the law.

10. *To deepen understanding of language and culture.* Languages can be used in education to introduce cultures of other times and places, to open new views of reality, or to give insights into human nature.[9]

Clearly, bilingual education serves at least two groups of students: those who wish to learn a second language by choice and those who must learn it if they are to prosper within the educational system and later in the world outside. In Canada, for instance, more and more anglophone parents are enrolling their children in French–English bilingual programs. There is no pressure on them to do so, but presumably they see some economic, educational, social or political advantage in the programs for their children. The children of indigenous or immigrant minorities, on the other hand, must master French or English or both if they are to take advantage of the opportunities available in the broader Canadian society. Indeed, if they do not get control of the language of instruction in the unilingual school system, they are at a great disadvantage. Bilingual education is also viewed as valuable for the children of seasonal migrant workers in that, by continuing to use their first language for academic purposes, they will be able to make the transition back to schooling in their own country better than if they had been using only the language of the receiving country. Bilingual education has therefore been viewed as enrichment for the children of the well-to-do dominant language group and as compensatory for the children of linguistic minorities, some of whom are also members of the low socio-economic group. It must be stressed, however, that children of linguistic minorities are not handicapped because they must master two languages; in fact they are enriched. They are only handicapped if the school makes insufficient effort to meet their particular needs.

In the United States concern for children with limited English from low-income homes resulted in the Bilingual Education Act of 1968 which was directed largely at Hispanic and native Americans. In 1974 the Act was refined and expanded to enlarge both the range of programs and the groups of children who qualified. Since then additional funds have been made available to evaluate the effectiveness of bilingual education programs. 'Yet, even with state and federal governments spending substantial amounts on bilingual education,' write Nancy Faires Conklin and Margaret A. Lourie, 'only one out of ten children with limited English was receiving any bilingual services in 1980. And budget cuts in the 1980s will probably reduce that proportion.'[10]

While justification for bilingual education can be gleaned from linguistics, psychology and sociology as well as from education, social attitudes, often based solely in emotion, remain powerful determiners of the kind of education provided to children. Many people in the English-speaking world still feel threatened when they hear a language other than their own spoken in their community. The desire to make everyone 'just like us' is very strong and it may well be many years before people can openly enjoy each others' linguistic and cultural diversity. Hence, attempts to mount bilingual education programs will continue to meet opposition either from those who see diversity as threatening, or from those who will not recognize the capacity of children to master two languages, or from those whose political or economic status might be undermined by better-educated members of minority groups.

ENGLISH AS A SECOND LANGUAGE

Anyone who has lived in a country not knowing the language of that country is well aware of the isolation that surrounds them. There are people everywhere, but no meaningful communication takes place on topics of mutual interest. The individual misses out on social, political, educational and vocational opportunities. But the community also loses. All people have something to give from the wealth of their knowledge and experiences, and for non-English-speaking children and adults living in an English-speaking environment, ESL programs are the means by which they can move from isolation to participation, benefiting both themselves and the community. The term 'second language' is, of course, a misnomer in cases where the learner already speaks three or four languages. What the term does, however, is to emphasize that the learner will be learning English in an English-speaking environment and will be using English in day-to-day living; that is, English will probably have equal use with the learner's first language, though not necessarily in the same settings. For instance, immigrants to one of the English-speaking countries will need a high level of fluency in English if they are to enter into the educational, social, vocational, professional, economic, and political life of the host community, but within their own homes, churches or ethnic communities their heritage languages will prevail.

ESL programs and bilingual education are compatible but not synonymous. Bilingual education uses English and another language, for example, English and Spanish, and where the Spanish-speaking students are largely immigrants English will be taught as the second language. What bilingual education does that ESL does not do is to consciously and concurrently take responsibility for helping children to maintain their first language. But this is only possible in situations where there are enough children speaking or learning to speak those two target languages and no others. In some communities a number of different ethnic groups live in close proximity, so that within a class ten or more languages may be represented. Clearly, in such cases, bilingual education is not feasible, and the alternative is ESL. While ESL teachers cannot teach the various ancestral languages in class, they can encourage the students to attend heritage language classes which may be offered in school time or after school or at the weekends. The aim of ESL classes for children is not, however, simply to teach them English and to integrate them into the mainstream, it is also to assist them in making the adjustment to a new culture as represented both in the school and in the community outside.

During the last twenty years ESL classes in the major immigrant-receiving countries such as Britain, the United States, Canada and Australia, have grown considerably in quantity, quality, and respectability. However, some people question whether providing English language training to non-English-speaking children is enough or whether education systems should not do more. Glyn Lewis writes:

> In a bilingual society, the minority student needs as a minimum to be able to speak two languages, his mother tongue and the lingua franca. The optimum provision is an education that is as comprehensive and as satisfying to members of a minority as the mainstream system is to the English-speaking student. Between the minimum and maximum requirements lies the need for providing an education that ensures, through the use of the mother tongue, that the student has an equal chance to 'achieve' academically. The minimum requirement involves simply the inclusion of an additional subject – English as a second language. The intermediate requirement involves simply substituting the mother tongue instead of, or in addition to, English as a teaching language. The maximum requirement takes us beyond individual programs and involves the establishment of an *alternative system* of education, like that provided in such bilingual countries as Belgium, Wales, Ireland, South Africa and Malaysia.[11]

In parts of the English-speaking world today even Lewis's minimum requirement is not met.

STANDARD ENGLISH AS A SECOND DIALECT

While some children come to school not speaking the language of instruction, others speak it but their dialect is sufficiently different from that used in the classroom to impede their progress. While it is certainly the role of the school to help children expand and refine their language, non-acceptance by teachers of the speech patterns their students learned in their home communities can adversely affect the students' attitudes towards and expectations of the school as well as their self-concepts. When it is school, district or ministry policy to be flexible in allowing variety in language use and usage in schools while students are assisted in becoming familiar with the standard form of the language, particularly its written form, alienation towards school is considerably diminished.

There are still some members of the public and unfortunately of the teaching profession who believe that a non-standard way of speaking, which they term 'bad grammar', automatically identifies the speaker as ignorant, incompetent and guilty of corrupting the English language. These people usually fail to discriminate between those who speak a non-standard dialect and those who are, for whatever reason, incompetent users of whatever dialect they speak. Black English, West Indian English, Scottish English, Nigerian English, Cockney English and the other versions of English are, as linguistic systems, all capable of allowing their speakers to think what they want to think and to say what they want to say. But a speaker can, of course, be an incompetent user of standard English or any of its non-standard dialects; the fault, however, lies with the speaker, not with the dialect.

Children soon realize on entering school that their language is not the same as that of their teacher. As young children cannot – and should not – be expected to change their speech patterns overnight, it is the teacher who must change. Conklin and Lourie report on a court decision which affected the teaching of non-standard speakers. They write:

> In 1979 a US District Court mandated that the Ann Arbor,
> Michigan, School Board devise a plan for helping teachers to
> identify Black English Vernacular speakers and to use that
> knowledge in teaching BEV speakers to read standard English. This
> precedent-setting decision implies that, to offer equal educational
> opportunity to nonstandard-speaking children, schools must take
> active steps to ensure that teachers understand the children's home
> dialect and use that knowledge in the teaching of standard English.
> Presumably, similar orders could be applied to those who teach
> speakers of any nonstandard variety, such as Appalachian English
> or Spanish-influenced English.[12]

Many educators and parents believe that the goal of bidialectism is a sound one: bidialectal students would, like their bilingual peers, have access to the world of standard English while maintaining ties with their home community through their non-standard dialect. However, others question whether, if non-standard dialects are not inferior to the standard dialect, students should be required either to add another dialect or change their speech patterns; that is, they argue that students have a right to their own form of English. It is at this point that a political and a pedagogical question meet once more in education.

MODERN OR FOREIGN LANGUAGE TEACHING

Modern or foreign language teaching bridges the gap between issues which affect primarily children and those which affect adults. On every continent in schools, colleges and universities world languages are taught as subjects. The choice of which foreign language is to be taught, however, may have political overtones. In eastern bloc countries the language taught is Russian (often as a second language) followed by English. In countries allied to the western bloc, the most popular language taught is English. When the People's Republic of China broke with the USSR, schools and universities switched from Russian to English.

The objectives of a modern language program may be to give the students either a speaking or reading/writing knowledge of the language or both, depending on the students' goals, as well as an introduction to a new culture. The opportunity to enter a number of careers ranging from diplomat to hotel worker, fashion buyer to missionary, foreign correspondent to tour guide may depend on a knowledge of one or more modern languages. Hence access to modern language programs can significantly affect people's livelihoods.

ENGLISH AS A FOREIGN LANGUAGE

No nation can isolate itself from world trade and world politics. Some of its citizens must master at least one of the major languages if that country is going to be an active member of the international community, and in many parts of the world that language will be English. 'English is known by some persons in virtually every country in the world,' write Conrad and Fishman. They provide figures showing that 76.7 percent of secondary students throughout the world are enrolled in English classes. Some of these students will complete their higher education in English and perhaps study abroad. English is used as the sole official language in twenty-one countries and as the co-official language in another sixteen countries. English is widely used in the media in countries where English is the mother tongue and where it is not.[13]

Developing countries in particular need people familiar with modern science and technology. This may require study abroad in an English-speaking country. Ultimately, knowledge of principles and practices is of more benefit to developing nations than the acquisition of material goods through foreign-aid programs. The choice of who goes abroad and what they study is, of course, a political issue. Teachers engaged in teaching English as a Foreign Language know that the students struggling with English in their class today may tomorrow be leaders of the nation in trade, politics, religion, education, science or technology. They are the elite, chosen perhaps from the elite, perhaps from all segments of the society.

The demand from countries around the world for native speakers of English as language teachers has resulted in the growth of a body of 'foreign experts' teaching overseas. Organizations such as the British Council and VSO (Volunteers Service Overseas), or the United States' various government and university-sponsored programs and the Peace Corps, or Canada's CIDA (Canadian International Development Agency) and CUSO (Canadian University Service Overseas) programs have supplied many EFL teachers to developing nations. Some people, however, question whether it is ethical for 'foreign experts' to teach abroad in countries where they believe the use to which the knowledge may be put is not in accord with principles of human dignity, liberty and justice. The teaching of English as a Foreign Language is not, therefore, without political ramifications.

ENGLISH FOR SPECIAL/SPECIFIC PURPOSES

Adults learning English as a second language are usually seeking competence for one of three purposes: vocational or professional employment, social interaction, or further education. At issue again are the questions covering what courses will be offered to whom by whom.

It was obvious to host nations that newly arrived adult immigrants required some mastery of English if they were to enter the workforce, and so classes providing basic English syntax and vocabulary were mounted, often at no cost to the students. However, after a few months or when the immigrants found jobs – any jobs, not necessarily those for which they had been trained in their home country – access to language training ceased. From then on immigrants were – and in many places today still are – expected to find their own way up the ladder from dishwasher to technician or professional, or whatever their previous education had made of them. Consequently, some language centers now offer courses specifically for nurses, or carpenters, or business people to give them the special English skills they need for the kind of employment they are seeking.

For years immigrant women remained closeted in their homes.

Because they were not seen as breadwinners, they did not have access to English language classes supposed to lead to employment. In addition, some were prohibited by the norms of their cultures from participating in fee-paying ESL classes. No one can live fully when isolated from the community. As their need – indeed, their plight – became obvious to community workers, classes were started specifically for immigrant women, for mothers and small children, and for senior citizens (often women). English for social interaction became recognized as an important component of the resettlement of immigrants. However, because such programs are not linked directly to employment and hence to the economy of the country, funding for these programs has not usually been as easy to obtain as funding for programs for vocational training.

The third purpose which English-language-training programs serve is that of furthering the education of non-English-speaking adults. At one end of the continuum are those who are illiterate or semi-literate in their first language and who need to become at least functionally literate in English if they are to cope in what is essentially a literate society. At the other end are those who hope to enter an English-medium college or university. In between are those seeking upgrading in academic or vocational skills and knowledge.

The issue facing host countries is whether to provide specialized language training and, if so, whether to charge students or to provide it free. If a host country intends to offer citizenship to immigrants after, say, a three or five year waiting period, it has a definite stake in ensuring that newcomers master the official language sufficiently well that they can obtain satisfactory employment, and hence pay taxes and participate in community affairs. If, however, a host country intends that migrant workers shall return to their homelands at the end of a period of employment, it may be that the less encouragement the workers are given to integrate the better.

WORLDWIDE LITERACY

A worldwide educational goal, still far from being achieved, is that of literacy for all. Literacy opens the door to further education in the arts and sciences. It also opens the door to participation in community affairs. Lenin (1918) maintained that 'an illiterate person is outside politics and he has to be taught his ABC. Without this there can be no politics.'[14] The failure of nations to provide access to literacy skills equally to all citizens means that some will unquestionably be oppressed and depressed. The writings of Paulo Freire and Ivan Illich have dealt at length with the ways in which lack of educational opportunity can adversely affect the lives of millions of peasants all over the world.

The community as beneficiary

But providing literacy skills in areas where there are perhaps no written versions of the language, or where literate people are few, or where the economy is weak is a formidable task. Language planners have to decide which written-symbol system will be best to introduce, given the nature and number of dialects spoken in the community and the written system(s) of the language(s) of wider communication in which the students' post-secondary education may take place. They have to decide how best to employ the few literate people to teach the much larger number of illiterates. And overarching these two issues will be that of finding funds for a massive literacy campaign.

In education, language policy is normally made by governments in response to political and pedagogical issues. It remains true, though perhaps unfortunate, that in most instances political expediency will outweigh pedagogical needs resulting in short- rather than long-term planning. Therefore, no matter how good a case language planners make for the inclusion of a particular language program within the total curriculum of an institution on pedagogical grounds, unless they can show how the program benefits the community or nation politically or economically they may have trouble getting the program approved.

Yet in bilingual and multilingual communities, the needs of majority and minority groups are different. To ignore the needs of either is to create disparate groups rather than to integrate them. Alternative systems of education, and there are many possible models, by incorporating different language-teaching programs could ensure that a minimum number of children and adults are linguistically handicapped and a maximum number linguistically enriched.

Linguistic and cultural heritage maintenance

The maintenance of heritage languages and cultures again raises both political and pedagogical questions. Is it politically wise to allow minority groups to reinforce their separateness through maintenance of their ethnic language? Is it pedagogically sound to reinforce the mother tongue of minority children who will be educated in a different language in a unilingual school system? Some years ago the answers to both questions would have been negative. However, the concept of cultural pluralism or multiculturalism is slowly gaining acceptance and with it the acceptance of multilingualism. Today the answers are increasingly positive.

Juan Cobarrubias writes: 'The issue of the official attitudes towards linguistic minorities has not been stressed sufficiently in the literature. It is not only important to our understanding of the nature of language rights but also shows how language-status planning issues are related to political issues.' He goes on to offer a possible taxonomy of official attitudes towards minority languages:

1. attempting to kill the language;
2. letting a language die;
3. unsupported coexistence;
4. partial support of specific language functions;
5. adoption as an official language.[15]

Minority ethnic groups cannot be treated alike by language planners because they differ in some fundamental ways. One of these is the nature of their contact with the majority group. Carol Eastman writes:

> For example, a group that is on an equal footing with another group from the point of view of power, is incorporated with that group, has many people in it, has been in the area a long time, is socially mobile, is highly acculturated, and is highly industrialized is hardly likely to undergo language shift! In contrast consider American Indian groups in most of the United States from the perspective of these features. Most of them have a plus value only for having been in the area for a long time, and some are highly acculturated; however, for all other features they have negative values. No wonder that the American Indian languages are rapidly dying out. [16]

In addition, minority groups differ from each other in the following ways:
– their family and social structures;
– their child-rearing practices;
– their value systems;
– their degree of economic development and hence security;
– the influence they can exert in the political sphere;
– their past histories;
– the geographical distribution of the group;
– the extent to which their language is used by all generations;
– the functions for which language is used in the community and the degree to which these differ from the functions for which the dominant language is used;
– the amount of linguistic reinforcement from other speakers of the language located outside the community;
– the determination of the group to maintain their language.

While heritage language programs have had some success in giving students some oral and written skills and some background in the culture, they have not been so successful in infusing in all students a desire to retain the language and to use it in their daily lives within the speech community. Urban children in particular simply do not see retention of the heritage language as necessary or desirable. The degree of language maintenance seems to be greater in those ethnic groups that have distanced themselves somewhat from the mainstream of society either geographically, socially, culturally, psychologically or institutionally.

However, children who grow up speaking their ancestral language have not only a ready channel of communication to their elders, often the source of cultural values and tradition, but an additional means of intellectual development and self-expression. They also acquire a sense of group identity, and while they may at a later date reject that identity, the knowledge of who they are and where they have come from prevents that sense of rootlessness, of living in limbo, experienced by those who do not know their personal or group past. For the group itself, the maintenance of their language provides a sense of continuity. It represents their ethnic affiliation and is a symbol of their separateness from other groups, a separateness which some see as threatening national unity. But for nations which are past fearing cultural diversity, multilingualism is regarded as an economic and social resource.

1.4 The language-planning process

The language-planning process must take the following factors into account:

Linguistic factors e.g. whether a written form is available;
Sociological factors e.g. the status of the language in society;
Economic factors e.g. the cost of the program;
Political factors e.g. the possible effect on national unity;
Cultural factors e.g. attitudes towards cultural pluralism;
Psychological factors e.g. motivation to learn another language;
Religious factors e.g. conflicting value systems.

Joan Rubin has outlined four steps that must be followed in formulating and carrying out a plan designed to address a particular language problem such as deciding which language shall be used as the medium of instruction in education or in the legislature, or to assist in economic development, or to promote national unity. Her four steps are summarized below:

1. *Fact finding*. The planner must determine the needs of the client, know something about the sociolinguistic setting in which the plan is to be implemented, determine the patterns of usage, and be aware of how the plan relates to other socio-economic and political processes.

2. *Establishing goals, strategies and outcomes.* The planner must identify the problems and assign them a degree of priority. Goals may be set at various levels: a legislature may establish general goals, an agency or institution more specific goals, the implementors may define the goals in terms of the local situation. Strategies are worked out to meet the stated goals. If outcomes are established in advance, some sort of evaluation of the strategies can be made.
3. *Implementation.* Implementation involves the mobilization of material and human resources, the motivation and supervision of those working in the program and the sequencing and coordination of different aspects of the program.
4. *Evaluation.* The plan is monitored and specific aspects are evaluated. The planner must determine whether the actual outcomes match the predicted outcomes or whether the strategies should be modified.[17]

Language planners' clients may vary between a government agency, a school district, or a minority group, each with its own interests very much at heart. Language planners must at all times be aware of the political consequences of any plan they suggest; that is, will the plan which satisfies one group cause another to feel unjustly treated? Will the plan have the desired effect? For example, bilingual education programs may have mother-tongue maintenance as their goal, but once the students are fluent in the dominant language they may prefer to use it rather than the language of the more restricted minority group because of the wider social and vocational opportunities it opens up. The ultimate result of the program may not be language maintenance but language shift as the students move their allegiance from one language to the other.

Lewis points out that any language plan has to consider attitude:

> Any policy for language, especially in the system of education, has to take account of the attitude of those likely to be affected. In the long run, no policy will succeed which does not do one of three things: conform to the expressed attitudes of those involved; persuade those who express negative attitudes about the rightness of the policy; or seek to remove the causes of the disagreement. In any case knowledge about attitudes is fundamental to the formulation of a policy as well as to success in its implementation.[18]

1.5   Language-teaching programs

Within the field of language teaching there are many different programs which language planners may adopt to attain their goals. We will consider the following: EFL programs, modern language programs, ESL, bilingual education programs, vernacular language programs, and heritage language programs.

ENGLISH AS A FOREIGN LANGUAGE PROGRAMS

English is termed a 'foreign language' in those countries where the language spoken outside the classroom is not English. EFL programs begin in some countries in primary school and continue through college and university. The objectives of the programs may vary according to the age, ability and aims of the students, and the short- and long-term goals of the community or nation. For example, the objectives may be to give students a basic knowledge of spoken English, some simple reading and writing skills, and a little understanding of the culture of the English-speaking world; or the objectives may be to provide students with sufficient command of English so that they can read literature and research reports in English, conduct business transactions, or take part in international conferences carried on in English.

MODERN LANGUAGE PROGRAMS (OTHER THAN ENGLISH)

The age level at which modern language teaching begins varies widely from program to program. Some children may begin the acquisition of another language in an immersion program starting in elementary school; others may have to wait until secondary school before they may study the language as a subject two or three periods a week. While there have been many complaints regarding the failure of modern language programs to produce fluent speakers of the language, when the hours devoted to modern language study are compared to the hours children spend learning their first language it is apparent that the goal of fluency is rather unrealistic.

Courses in modern languages for adults are of two kinds: 1) college or university courses covering both language and literature, and 2) short courses designed to give the learners a smattering of the language for 'fun and travel'.

ENGLISH AS A SECOND LANGUAGE PROGRAMS

ESL programs for adults may be quite general, that is, they try to give the students some basic structures and vocabulary or they may be very specific. Under the rubric of ESP (English for Special/Specific Purposes) instructors teach job-oriented courses dealing with such topics as medicine, nursing, carpentry, forestry, agriculture, business administration, or hotel work. Other courses prepare students for advanced academic work or citizenship. Some programs take place in factories where employees' lack of facility in English constitutes a safety hazard to the group or blocks promotion for the individual. Special classes are mounted for women whose poor English keeps them housebound.

A variety of programs have been developed for ESL children. Their aim is often twofold: 1) to give the children enough English so that they can enter the mainstream of education, and 2) to assist them in adjusting to the new culture. Specifically, the most common programs found in schools are as follows:

1. *Reception classes.* All students are ESL. They remain in the class until the teacher feels they are ready to be mainstreamed.
2. *Half-day classes.* The students spend half the day in the ESL class and half in regular subject classes.
3. *Withdrawal or pullout classes.* Students are withdrawn from their regular subject classes for one or more periods a week for special English language instruction in small groups, perhaps in an English Language Center.
4. *Transitional classes.* The students cover the same content as is covered in the regular class but the language component is adapted to suit their language-proficiency level.
5. *Special education ESL classes.* These classes are for students who have learning disabilities in addition to speaking limited English.
6. *Pre-employment ESL classes.* These classes are for students who need functional and vocational English to help them enter the workforce.

BILINGUAL EDUCATION PROGRAMS

Joshua A. Fishman describes four categories of bilingual education involving the mother tongue and the official language. These are summarized below:

Type 1: Transitional bilingualism. The students' first language is used in the early grades to the extent necessary to allow them to 'adjust to school' and/or 'master subject matter' until the second language is developed to the point that it alone can be used as the medium of instruction. Then the first language is dropped.
Type 2: Monoliterate bilingualism. Aural–oral skills are developed in both languages. Literacy skills are developed only in the official language, not in the mother tongue.
Type 3: Biliterate bilingualism, partial. Fluency and literacy are sought in both languages, but literacy in the mother tongue is restricted to certain subject matter, generally that related to the ethnic group and its cultural heritage.
Type 4: Biliterate bilingualism, full. Students develop all skills in both languages in all domains.[19]

James Cummins suggests that children should not be mainstreamed after an initial two or three years in a primary bilingual program. He states '...there is no educational support for the assumption that children should be switched to a majority language program in order to develop adequate literacy skills in the majority language'. He points out that students in bilingual programs begin to pull ahead of their monolingual peers in the later grades of elementary school by which time literary skills in both languages have become well established.[20]

VERNACULAR LANGUAGE PROGRAMS

Vernacular language teaching is not necessarily synonymous with bilingual education. In a number of countries the first three years of the children's education is carried on mainly in the vernacular while the second language is taught as a subject but not used as a medium of instruction. Then for the following three years the second language is phased in until it becomes the sole medium of instruction. Because of the importance of vernacular language teaching in young children's cognitive and affective development, it is imperative that it be done well.

HERITAGE LANGUAGE PROGRAMS

Heritage language programs are usually of two kinds: those supported by the authorities and incorporated into the school system; and those run by ethnic societies or by indigenous group councils. Programs run by minority groups take place either in the early evening after school hours or on Saturday mornings. In the past textbooks were often old or non-existent and teachers were untrained. Recent interest, however, in ethnic language maintenance has resulted in some government and private money being made available for the development of up-to-date curricula and materials and for training courses for teachers.

A few minority groups have set up their own separate schools, often bilingual, where their own language is used for a considerable part of the school day. These schools are often associated with a particular religion, for example, Hebrew language schools for Jewish children, or German language schools for Mennonite children.

1.6 The benefits of language teaching to individuals and the community

Formal education plays a substantial role in assisting people to build worthwhile lives and to contribute to society. It has, therefore, both a personal and a social relevance: it serves individuals and the community.

The development of first and second language skills in children and adults is the key to thoughtful behavior and to good personal relationships among people of different linguistic and cultural backgrounds. Control of language opens the door to various vocations, to an exploration of the physical world, to great literature and to great minds, and helps to produce an informed and reflective citizenry. However, while all this may be true, it means nothing if the community which is asked to supply the resources does not see language-teaching programs as responding to some individual and community needs.

If the community is to be fully aware of the benefits accruing to it through the various language-teaching programs offered in its institutions in order that it will continue to support them, teachers must be able to articulate the value of the work they are doing. It is not difficult to justify to the tax-paying public the value of teaching basic literacy or numeracy skills. It is more difficult to justify language-teaching programs: first, because some issues surrounding language teaching involve people's deep emotions rather than their reason; and, second, because the per-ceived past failure of programs to produce fluent users of the language causes people to question the wisdom of throwing good money after bad. The fact that the objectives of the programs were often far beyond attainment is not always understood by the critics.

In order that the benefits may become apparent, justification for language-teaching programs must include some statements about the linguistic needs of the individual, the community or the nation to which the program is responding. As has been suggested in the preceding sections, there are a number of reasons why a particular program should be mounted depending on the issue it is addressing. Benefits felt by the individual, the community or the nation will therefore vary according to the goal of the program. However, language planners have at all times to be aware that where there is a 'winner' there may also be a 'loser'. Groups with little power such as minority ethnic groups, religious groups or tribal groups may not benefit from decisions made in favor of political, military, occupational, industrial or institutional groups.

The following is a list of some of the benefits which the individual, the community, or the nation may derive from language programs:

The individual
– a sense of self-worth
– a sense of personal identity
– a good attitude towards speakers of other languages
– broader cultural horizons
– fluency in two languages
– literacy in two languages
– maintenance of the first language
– continued intellectual development as the student shifts from one
   language to another

29

The community as beneficiary

- an equal opportunity for a sound education
- an enriched education
- an opportunity to enter a post-secondary institution at home or abroad
- an improved opportunity to enter the workforce
- wider career possibilities
- an improved opportunity to enter the social, religious or political life of the community
- the fulfilment of the language component of citizenship requirements
- greater ease when travelling

The community
- citizens who contribute to and participate in the life of the community through their ability to communicate in a common language
- an educated citizenry who can draw on ideas presented in another language
- a language-proficient workforce
- successful integration of newcomers into the community
- improved links between the unilingual school system and minority-group parents
- greater flexibility of communication between the generations and between members of different speech communities
- the maintenance of minority languages and cultures, and the preservation of a community's values and customs
- public acknowledgement of the linguistic make-up of the community
- public validation of particular languages and cultures
- greater toleration for and appreciation of other languages and cultures resulting in greater harmony in the community

The nation
- national unity
- the ability to govern through one or more commonly understood languages
- the ability to offer services to its citizens in languages they understand
- an educated citizenry able to work in two languages where necessary
- access to the recent findings of science and technology published in other languages
- increased industrialization through a knowledge of modern science and technology
- the ability to compete in international trade markets
- the ability to engage in dialogue with other nations

While the three lists above are not exhaustive, they may serve to stimulate language teachers to think of other ways in which their profession is of value to the public.

Activities

1. Examine three language-teaching programs offered in your community. What are their aims and objectives? What issues do they address?
2. Investigate the relationship of language and national unity in one of the developing nations. What solution has been adopted?
3. Give both sides of a language-teaching issue facing your community. If you were a language planner, what program would you advise the community to implement?
4. Using the list of benefits outlined under *The individual*, *The community*, and *The nation* as a starting point, prepare a report on the benefits to be derived from a particular language program with which you are familiar.

2 The community as resource

This chapter will describe different kinds of communities which affect or are affected by second-language-teaching programs, and will suggest ways of locating and using community resources.

2.1 Overview

While the community is eventually the beneficiary of what goes on in educational institutions, it is also their prime resource. In addition to funding institutions through taxes levied on it, the community provides a wide range of human and material resources which help institutions to accomplish their objectives.

We tend to forget that before schooling became compulsory, the community was the teacher of all its children and adults. Today the education, socialization, and acculturation of people, young and old, continues to take place in a variety of community settings, including schools, colleges and universities, using a variety of resources. Recently there has been considerable support for having students go back into the community to serve it and to learn from it, and conversely for having people from the community bring their knowledge and skills into the institutions. The role of the teacher has changed from that of the omniscient knower and sole imparter of information to that of facilitator of learning, which has resulted in bringing the community and its students closer together through the use of community resources.

The first section of this chapter (2.2) will describe different kinds of communities that impinge in different ways on language teaching. The next section (2.3) will examine how language is used in these communities and the relationship of the target language to other languages. This will be followed (2.4) by an investigation of the decision-making process which affects, directly or indirectly, what resources will be made available to the various institutions and in what quantities. The final sections will consider (2.5) how to discover the distinctive features of a community, and (2.6) how to locate and use these resources.

2.2 Kinds of communities

A community is more than just a group of people. An ideology, a relationship, a function, a purpose, a situation, an event – something binds its members together. A community may be a social, political, economic or administrative unit; or it may be an ideological, ecological or linguistic unit. It may be enclosed by narrow or broad geographic boundaries. A community may be a formal, legal, long-lasting unit or an informal, ad hoc, short-term unit. Interaction may occur horizontally among peers or vertically through a hierarchy. Cohesion between members of the group may be very tight or very loose.

Different aspects of language teaching affect or are affected by different communities. These communities will be categorized under three headings: geo-political communities, common interest communities, and professional communities.

GEO-POLITICAL COMMUNITIES

Geo-political communities lie within certain fixed physical boundaries and perform some political function. ('Political' is used here in its broad sense of concern for the well-being of its citizens.) The following are geo-political communities:

1. neighborhoods, including reservations and ghettos
2. school districts
3. electoral districts, municipal and rural
4. counties, provinces and states
5. nations

Each of these geo-political communities has fairly distinct physical boundaries. The inhabitants know where one neighborhood or one county or one nation begins or ends. In some cases two different geo-political communities may overlap partially or fully; that is, a school district and a municipal electoral district may include some or all of the same voters within their boundaries. While these various communities may work cooperatively, there is obviously a hierarchy: the nation can impose its will on the neighborhood. But that does not preclude the neighborhood through pressure and lobbying tactics from influencing the national will. Each of these communities possesses resources – financial, material, and human – which can. be made available to or withheld from educational institutions.

COMMON INTEREST COMMUNITIES

Within geo-political communities and reaching across their boundaries are common interest communities – groups of people who share a common history, experience, language, culture, or political or religious ideology. Some of these groups are as follows:

1. social communities such as families
2. speech communities having a common language or dialect

3. minority groups whether defined by ethnicity or socio-economic status
4. ideological groups such as religious, political or pressure groups

Group solidarity within these communities has its roots in ideas, emotions, and sentiments which transcend neighborhood, county, state, provincial or national boundaries. The resources of these communities are usually made available to educational institutions either to maintain the status quo or to change it; that is, these communities are concerned with the quality of life seen in its historical and ideological perspective.

PROFESSIONAL COMMUNITIES

Professional communities are defined here as those which are directly concerned with some aspect of language teaching, such as the following:

1. the classroom
2. the institutional community
3. teacher-training institutions
4. organizations of students, parents and/or teachers

Professional communities are usually fairly close-knit. Most of the people are known to the rest of the community except in the case of national organizations where only the leaders are well-known across the country. While each community is distinct from the other communities, they all have in common a desire to see that students receive a good education. One would expect, therefore, a high degree of mutual support and cooperation among the professional communities, but unfortunately, this is not always so. Resources available from the communities are closely related to the teaching/learning situation.

Any person may be simultaneously a member of more than one geo-political community, common interest community, or professional community.

There are many forces outside a community which may destroy it, modify it, or solidify it. These are often political, economic or ideological in nature. Any one of the following, for example, can change the character of a community:
− a technological revolution or rapid industrialization
− a change in political ideology
− increased mobility of the population
− a movement from rural to urban living
− social disorder and crime
− an economic boom or recession
− political instability
− a change in social values and beliefs

– population decline or explosion
– war or the fear of war
– any new idea whose time has come
Tension within communities occurs because of the simultaneous desire
of different members of the community, on the one hand to seek change
and on the other hand to resist it. Part of this tension may lie in the fact
that while on the surface individuals and communities may appear to
have common problems, there may be some fundamental differences due
to past history and experiences which are not apparent until a major
problem is encountered.

2.3   Language use in the community

Most people take language for granted. Few people, unless they are
language teachers, are conscious of the many and diverse functions for
which language is employed in a community. In a unilingual community,
one language is employed for all functions, but in a bilingual or
multilingual community, one language may be used for some functions
and another language for other functions. The functions for which a
language is used in a community affect the status of the language. The
official language, that is, the language of government, business and
education, will, in all probability, have a higher status than a language
used only in the home. Resources may therefore be more readily
forthcoming for teaching the official language than for teaching the
minority language unless maintenance or expansion of the minority
language is seen as being of benefit to the community. The following
are some functions for which language is used at some time by most
people:

1. *Family life.* Language is used in the home for a variety of personal
   encounters and interactions. In bilingual or multilingual societies, the
   home may be the last bastion for the preservation of a minority
   language.
2. *Daily business.* Language is used in the marketplace to facilitate the
   exchange of goods and services. Local business may be carried on
   in minority languages, but business carried on across speech
   boundaries may use a language of wider communication.
3. *Public education.* Language is the vehicle through which teachers
   teach and students learn. Minority and/or majority languages may
   be used depending on the official policy adopted.
4. *Public administration.* Rules and regulations are transmitted to
   people through oral and written language, usually in the official
   language.

5. *The media.* Radio, television and the press disseminate information through oral and written language. Modern technology has made it possible for people to hear, view and read news from around the world in a variety of languages.
6. *Cultural maintenance.* Culture, including ethnicity and religion, is rooted in language which is used to describe, explain and practice the value systems and traditions of the culture. While cultures do not necessarily die out when the language is lost, they change significantly.
7. *The arts.* Certain forms of the arts, such as literature, theater, opera, and folk music use language as part of the medium of expression. Because art transcends politics, economics and nationalism, the language of its expression crosses international boundaries.
8. *Industrial development.* The exchange of ideas and techniques in science and technology occur through language. Scientists and technicians in both developed and developing countries often use more than one language of wider communication in order to facilitate the flow of ideas.
9. *International trade and politics.* Language is used in international affairs whether these are concerned with the flow of trade or the subtleties of politics. The language of wider communication chosen as the medium will depend on who the participants are and their relationship.

The status a language holds in a community depends on who speaks and writes it, when, where, and for what purpose. Programs teaching high-status languages can usually obtain more resources more easily than those teaching low-status languages. There is, of course, nothing intrinsic in any language that makes it high-status or low-status. It is people who decide the place each language holds in society. As was pointed out in chapter 1, a language which is the medium of instruction in the schools, is widely spoken in the community, is used for government and commerce, and has a large body of literature extending back centuries will probably have a higher status than one which is not used as the medium of instruction or for government or commerce, is spoken by a handful of people and has no written system. The following questions may help to pinpoint the status a particular target language (the language being taught) has in a particular institution or community:

1. Is the target language the medium of instruction in the institution?
2. Does the target language have at least equal prestige in the local community with the learners' first language?
3. Is the target language seen by the learners as either desirable or necessary for academic, vocational or recreational purposes?

4. Will the target language be used for post-secondary education by the learners?
5. Does the target language have its own body of literature?
6. Is the target language widely spoken in the vicinity of the institution offering the program?
7. Is the target language spoken by the dominant group in the nation?
8. Is the target language spoken widely throughout the world?
9. Is the target language used to conduct the business of the national government?
10. Is the target language used in international politics?
11. Is the target language used by the media and the entertainment field?
12. Is the target language used for trading with other nations?
13. Is the target language associated with a culture that arouses positive feelings in the learners?
14. Is the target language flourishing or dying?

If positive answers exceed negative answers, it is likely that the target language has reasonably high status and is receiving community support.

2.4   Decision-making within communities

Community involvement in educational issues can strengthen the ties between educational institutions and citizens, helping them to develop jointly a better understanding of problems and solutions, binding them together with a sense of purpose. Formal education plays a substantial role in assisting people to build worthwhile lives and to contribute to society. But in order to reap the benefits, the larger community must make an investment in education through financial, material and human resources. The benefits communities receive from education depend on the magnitude and kind of investment made and the use to which the educational system puts the investment. Inadequate resources poorly administered will produce inadequate benefits. It should, therefore, be a matter of concern to members of geo-political, common interest and professional communities that decisions to make available to or withhold resources from educational institutions are made in the best interests of both the students and the communities.

Decisions may be made through coercion or consensus, that is, through power or influence. Power is the ability to *cause* others to do what we want them to do. It has its base in authority whether political, legal or physical. Influence is the ability to *persuade* others to do what we want them to do. It has its base in mutual trust and respect. Decision-making may lie in the hands of a few people who make all the decisions in all areas of the issue or it may lie with a number of people who have power in different areas. Those who wish to be part of the decision-making process or at least to influence the process must identify the power structure and the channels of communication through which ideas pass.

John Galbraith, in his book *The Anatomy of Power*, distinguishes between three different kinds of power:

> Condign power threatens the individual with something physically or emotionally painful enough so that he foregoes pursuit of his own will or preference in order to avoid it.

> Compensatory power offers the individual a reward or payment sufficiently advantageous or agreeable so that he (or she) foregoes pursuit of his own preference to seek the reward instead.[1]

> While condign and compensatory power are visible and objective, conditioned power, in contrast, is subjective; neither those exercising it nor those subject to it need always be aware that it is being exerted. The acceptance of authority, the submission to the will of others, becomes the higher preference of those submitting. This preference can be deliberately cultivated – by persuasion or education. This is explicit conditioning. Or it can be dictated by the culture itself; the submission is considered to be normal, proper, or traditionally correct. This is implicit conditioning.[2]

All three kinds of power are exercised in our world today, and depending on the use to which they are put, they may hinder or enhance the passage of educationally-sound policies. (These ideas will be explored further in chapters 3 and 4.)

2.5   Finding out about communities

Communities are not identical. They are established in different places at different times for different reasons. Educators who want to help communities to build better lives for their people must develop an understanding of the specific community they are concerned with, its needs, its modes of operating, its strengths and weaknesses, and its resources. Outsiders who try to force their will on a community may upset the balance of power which has been developed over the years. Decisions arrived at through consensus within a community have a better chance of success than those imposed from outside. But in order to work with a community to help it decide what programs to mount and what resources to allocate, educators must first know the community.

Assessing various components of a community is a necessary prelude to helping its members solve their problems. A survey of a particular community undertaken through interviews, examination of reports, and observations might have all or some of the following objectives:

1. to determine who lives or works in the community, their social, economic, political, educational or religious backgrounds; the racial, ethnic or class composition of the community; the residential or migration patterns;
2. to develop some understanding of the community's needs, modes of operating, resources, strengths and weaknesses;
3. to determine the various power bases of groups and individuals; the patterns of interaction between these power bases and the rest of the community; the degrees of centralization and decentralization of power; and the representativeness of its appointed or elected officials;
4. to determine the kinds of services available to people, particularly educational and social services, and which groups do or do not have access to these services;
5. to develop an awareness of past history which has shaped the community into what it is today and provided it with structures which do or do not permit it to respond to changing needs and demands;
6. to determine major issues within the community which need to be addressed.

As both common interest and professional communities operate within and across geo-political communities, information on geo-political communities is of wide importance and concern. Many of the following dimensions of a geo-political community should therefore be known to any educator or educational institution seeking to harness community resources for educational purposes:

1. *Population*
   - density of population in the designated geographic area
   - decline or increase in population over the last few years
   - degree of stability or mobility of the population
   - percentage of people in different age ranges
   - percentage of people speaking different languages

2. *Social structure*
   - percentage of people in different income brackets or in different types of employment
   - geographic areas of high- and low-cost housing
   - types of family organizations
   - social services available

3. *Education*
   - percentage of people with elementary, secondary and university education

- numbers and kinds of educational institutions, their roles, membership, range of courses and organization
- processes by which decisions affecting education are made in the community

4. *Value systems*
   - nature of the dominant and sub-dominant value systems
   - long-standing traditions and customs
   - strength and range of the belief systems of religious groups

5. *Economic structure*
   - base of economic power
   - degree of economic stability
   - range of employment opportunities for members of majority and minority groups
   - numbers of unemployed people, their age range, education, and vocational or professional training

6. *Political structure*
   - base(s) of political power
   - political organizations, their objectives and membership
   - processes by which political decisions are made which affect the community

7. *Historical background*
   - reasons for the community's existence
   - major events which have helped to shape the community

Information on communities is available from different sources. The librarian at a public, college or university library is probably one of the best people to start with as he or she can usually point the researcher towards government reports, year books, census figures, and public and private agency reports and briefs. From then on the researcher is much like a private detective following every clue until the truth is discovered.

2.6 Locating community resources

There are six different kinds of resources that language teachers may want to locate:

1. *Funds.* Funds are usually needed to rent accommodation, pay salaries and purchase materials unless the community intends to run the language program entirely through volunteers and donated materials.
2. *People.* Individuals may act as volunteer teacher aides or as resource people supplying information on topics of concern and/or interest to the students, such as health, recreation, or vocational training.

3. *Materials*. Resource materials include not only textbooks and audio-visual aids purchased by the institution, but also pamphlets, films, posters, etc. which may be supplied free by the community.
4. *Sites*. While museums and art galleries are useful cultural resources, offices, construction sites, hotels and hospitals constitute the resources needed by those training for specific vocations.
5. *Agencies*. Public and private agencies act as resources to those seeking information or counselling on matters of personal or family concern.
6. *Activities*. Students learn more from taking part in an activity than just being told about it. Hence, an activity in which a student is interested is a resource for learning.

Teachers planning to use community resources can set up files using the headings above. As the contents will be added to or modified over the years, the format of the file should be one that permits changes to be easily made, for example, a loose-leaf binder, a set of cards, or a computer program. The first task, however, is to locate the resources.

Four strategies for locating resources are as follows:

1. Conduct a survey of the community by personal visits, telephone calls, or questionnaires to discover what, in a broad sense, is 'out there'.
2. Use that section of the telephone or local directory that lists individuals, companies, and agencies according to the service they offer. Contact those whose services may meet the learning needs of the students.
3. Build up a network of people knowledgeable about particular resources in the community of interest to students. Have them call whenever they find a new or better resource.
4. Notify the community by letter or through the local newspaper of the kind of resource needed by a particular group of students and hope for a good response.

As it is possible that someone has already compiled a list of resources, a check with the main library, an educational institution, or city hall may save duplication of effort. However, many language teachers may have to begin from scratch compiling their own lists. In such cases, casting the net wide through a comprehensive survey may turn up all that was originally sought and perhaps more. But before drawing up the survey, teachers should answer the following questions to ensure a sense of direction along with good organization:

– Why is the survey being made?
– What information might the survey turn up?
– Is a survey the best way to get at this information?
– Who will organize the survey and who will assist?

– How will the results be recorded?
– Who will use the results?
– How will the results be kept up-to-date?
– How will the survey be paid for?

Answers to these questions will indicate whether or not the survey is viable and should go ahead. The survey itself will cover the following items, information on which should be recorded in detail in the community resource file:

– what the resource is, its name, and where it is located;
– the time it is available for use, who may use it, in what numbers, and for how long;
– how the resource will help teachers and students and what its strengths and limitations are as a resource;
– the contact person;
– whether an appointment is needed in order to use/view the resource;
– how long a lead-time is necessary before the resource can be used/obtained;
– whether an orientation of teacher and/or students is necessary prior to using/viewing the resource;
– whether the individual/group must be supervised;
– the cost: entrance fee, charge for materials, honorarium, transportation, meals.

For language teachers, resources may center around some of the following topics:

– Community services
– Consumer education
– Employment
– Family life
– Other cultures
– Health
– Law
– Recreation
– Education
– Politics
– History

Once the community resource file has been established, the next step is to decide how to use the resources and for what purposes. The following are some suggestions:

Funds

While major funding is usually the responsibility of government or of the head of the institution, teachers should be aware that often there are minor grants available through government or private agencies which enable teachers to mount small pilot projects or to engage in classroom research.

There are two steps to obtaining such funds: 1) through persistent questioning of government officials and colleagues, draw up a list of possible funding agencies; 2) having obtained information on the type of proposals the agencies will fund, submit a carefully written application that is in accordance with their guidelines. Many proposals are turned down because they either are not congruent with the agency's objectives or they lack sufficient detail and clarity.

Volunteers

Volunteer classroom aides, particularly if they are bilingual, can be of great help to teachers. They can, for example,
- prepare materials for students to use in class;
- assist teachers in individualizing instruction;
- explain instructions and procedures to new students;
- relieve teachers of some non-teaching duties;
- assist in counselling students;
- give additional practice to students who need it;
- enrich students' experiences beyond what is normally possible;
- act as translators or interpreters;
- advise teachers on some of the language and cultural problems they or their students encounter.

Back in the community, volunteer classroom aides can
- help to build an understanding in the community of the problems facing language teachers and their students;
- strengthen school–community relations;
- encourage others to participate in the school's program.

Running a good volunteer program demands some initial preparation and organization as well as ongoing supervision. Both volunteers and teachers have to know what the goals of the program are and how their respective roles dovetail together. If goals and roles are not made clear at the outset, misunderstanding occurs which affects the quality of the interpersonal relationships being established.

A sequence for setting up a volunteer aide program is as follows:

1. Determine how volunteers can best assist teachers and students.
2. Establish the goals of the program.
3. Design the program – number of volunteers, where they will work, what they will do.
4. Establish what resources will be available to the volunteers.

5. Recruit and select the volunteers.
6. Provide them with an orientation to the program and teach any basic skills needed.
7. Train the teachers how to use volunteers effectively.
8. Allocate volunteers to classrooms and ensure that both teachers and volunteers are clear on the goals of the program and their roles in it.
9. Monitor the program and provide ongoing feedback to the teachers and volunteers.
10. Evaluate the program at the end of the term or at the termination of the program.
11. Provide the volunteers with some recognition of the service they have performed.

Colleagues

Within the institutional community, language teachers have a two-way relationship with other teachers: they can act as a resource for their colleagues who, in turn, can act as a resource for them.

THE LANGUAGE TEACHER AS A RESOURCE PERSON

1. *For other language teachers.* Unless the institution is totally given over to language teaching, language teachers may be very much in the minority, feeling, at times, somewhat isolated from others in the profession. Experienced teachers as well as inexperienced teachers need words of encouragement as well as the infusion of new ideas. Language teachers can help each other by
– discussing approaches, methods and techniques of language teaching;
– sharing ideas and materials that have proved to be effective in the classroom;
– providing support to new teachers or to colleagues in difficulty;
– cooperating in building curriculum and supporting materials;
– collaborating on ways to improve their programs.

2. *For teachers of other subjects.* The manner in which language teachers can be a resource for other subject-matter teachers will depend on the relationship of the target language to the language of instruction in the institution. Language teachers who are helping students to master the language of instruction (for example, ESL teachers) are, in a sense, performing a service for their colleagues. The speed and efficiency with which students master the target language will affect the speed and efficiency with which they will master the subject matter. Different subject areas, however, have their own special vocabularies and to a

lesser degree special syntax with perhaps an emphasis on a particular language function. Cooperation between language teachers and subject-matter teachers on what language items should be taught and how this can best be done can increase efficient language learning.

Modern language teachers, on the other hand, do not usually have the same pressures on them to produce fluent users of the language in a matter of months. They do, however, carry the same responsibility for helping to promote a deeper understanding of the multicultural nature of the world society. In this regard they can work with their colleagues in the other subject areas to show students that the knowledge we rely on today was not invented in one place at one time by one group, but that many races and nations have, over the centuries, contributed to the various subject-matter areas.

Language teachers can act as a resource for other subject-matter teachers by
- conducting a survey of the languages spoken by students and teachers to get a sense of the multicultural nature of the institution and the linguistic and cultural resources contained therein;
- providing an opportunity for other teachers to visit a language-teaching classroom to see the latest methods and techniques;
- assisting subject-matter teachers to examine the ways in which language (vocabulary, syntax, functions) is used uniquely in their subject;
- providing them, through formal and informal sessions, with an opportunity to explore their attitudes towards language and language learning;
- demonstrating that there is an important difference between learning to talk and talking to learn;
- providing an opportunity for subject-matter teachers to discover how language can be learned through subject matter and how subject matter can be learned through language teaching;
- cooperating in building a multicultural curriculum for use throughout the institution;
- planning together the best educational program for the students in attendance at the institution.

THE SUBJECT-MATTER TEACHER AS THE RESOURCE PERSON

Subject-matter teachers, particularly those who are experienced or who have been at the institution for some years, can act as a resource for language teachers by
- providing the new teacher with general information on the philosophy and organization of the institution, its rules and regulations, and the

make-up of the student body; and by providing information on the local community, its agencies, services, human and material resources;
– describing the language used to process the content of their subject matter;
– permitting the language teacher to observe the subject-matter class in action if this will assist language teaching/learning;
– inviting language students to demonstrate their language skills or their knowledge of other cultures in the subject-matter classroom when this is relevant;
– encouraging students in their classes to befriend those learning the language of instruction;
– supporting ethnic celebrations and festivals.

Guest speakers

Guest speakers whose roots lie in the culture and/or language being studied or who have a particular expertise can be a valuable resource to language teachers. These speakers may be foreign students, faculty who have taught overseas, immigrants, or expatriate teachers. The talk must, of course, suit the age and interest of the students both in its content and in the form of its delivery. Possible topics are as follows: food, clothing, festivals, customs, writing systems, kinship, education, economics, religion, politics, value systems, childrearing practices, history, travel. Guest speakers who are experts in a particular facet of local community life can be an important resource to ESL teachers. These might include policemen, firemen, public health nurses, employers, librarians, and recreation leaders.

Realia

When the students cannot be taken into the community, real-life materials can often be brought into the classroom. Advertising materials, application forms, report cards, bank statements, cheques, telephone directories, newspapers, signs and symbols can all act as focal points for learning language and culture simultaneously.

Field trips

Field trips to public places such as government institutions or commercial enterprises provide real-life experiences for students in both language and culture. Field trips may involve students from a minority group exploring aspects of the dominant or host community such as government service offices (post office, hospital, fire department, employment office), recreation or community centers and parks, the transportation system, museums, theaters, or local stores. Or the field trip may involve students from the dominant culture exploring a local minority culture through festivals, ceremonies, theater, restaurants, churches, cultural centers, heritage language schools, stores or factories.

To ensure a safe and successful field trip, the following points should be checked before the trip takes place:

1. legal requirements such as parental or other permission slips
2. transportation – route, time, cost
3. additional people to accompany the students
4. insurance coverage
5. health and safety factors
6. notices informing other teachers of the students' absence
7. letters to the individual/agency/firm confirming the day, time and objectives of the visit
8. preparation of the students for the field trip

Work–study programs

Students in pre-employment programs may need a combination of language-training and work experience. Some commercial enterprises are willing to provide such an opportunity to those who need it. As their names are rarely listed, language teachers are usually forced to find them out through friends and associates or perhaps through an appeal to the business community.

The arrangements made on behalf of a student should be in the form of a contract, so that the teacher, the student–employee, and the employer know exactly what is expected in terms of the hours to be worked, the days on which the student will attend, the nature of the work to be done, and the learning objectives. In addition, matters such as the pay scale, insurance, or safety factors should be clarified when applicable.

Student–community contact

In order to give students practice in using the target language in real-life situations, teachers can give students tasks to perform that will require them to talk face-to-face with members of the community. The test might be to get information, to purchase an article, or to make an appointment. On their return, students report on their experiences and get further help and support when needed. For students with limited language ability, teachers may want to set up a situation with a friend or associate to ensure that the early experience is a pleasurable one. But when the students are more fluent or more confident, teachers may well prefer to put them in unstructured situations and let them cope.

Local committees

Local committees can provide information on the community regarding both the current situation and what is being proposed for the future. In addition, local committees are often prepared to act as advocates for language teachers and their students once they are convinced of the need for their services in a specific cause. It is therefore worthwhile contacting groups such as parent–teacher or home–school associations, ethnic societies, churches, recreation or community centers, organizations of business people or service clubs as these will often give support to a program when they are convinced of its value.

Cultural and intercultural centers

Some centers promote understanding in only one culture and are run by a particular ethnic group. Intercultural centers bring a number of cultures together under one roof. Their broad objectives are to promote intercultural understanding, to encourage creativity in the arts, to provide information on specific cultures and on multiculturalism, to encourage feelings of pride in people's cultural identities, and to act as a resource for multicultural curriculum building. Most centers when approached are very willing to share their resources with language teachers and their students.

Community publications and services

In most communities there are usually a number of publications and services available to both teachers and students. Some of these may be available in languages other than the official language. Public libraries may have a list of the publications and services offered and the languages in which service can be obtained. Language teachers may find it helpful to keep on hand names and addresses, including the contact person, for the following:
– ethnic newspapers
– community information booklets
– information centers
– government offices (employment, medical or hospital insurance, driver's licence, etc.)
– counselling services
– translation or interpreter services
– travel agencies
– other educational institutions
– churches (different denominations)
– recreation or community centers

– child-care agencies
– hospitals and clinics
– private employment agencies
– libraries

A quick referral of the student by the teacher to the appropriate agency can often prevent small problems from becoming big ones.

Activities

1. Determine the important uses to which language is put in your community and any obstacles which hinder effective use of language.
2. Answer the question on pp. 36–7 with respect to your language-teaching program or one with which you are familiar; that is, assess the status of the target language in the institution and in the community in relation to other languages. Suggest reasons why the target language has high or low status in the community.
3. With a partner, conduct a survey of your local community to determine its make-up, its needs and its resources.
4. Conduct a survey of a particular resource (field trips, guest speakers, potential employers, services and publications, etc.). Publish your findings.
5. Collect realia (forms, advertising materials, signs, etc.) and decide how each could be used effectively in the language-teaching classroom.
6. Draw up a list of potential situations in the community where students could practice the target language with native speakers.

3 The community as control

This chapter will consider the influence of local community groups on language teaching and suggest ways in which teachers can get support for their programs.

3.1 Overview

In chapter 2 three different kinds of communities were identified: geo-political, common interest, and professional. Within these communities can be found a number of groups each one of which can affect language teaching in its own distinct way. Some groups, like the family, have long and enduring histories; others rise and fall in a matter of months. Some, like specific pressure groups, are primarily self-serving; others are other-serving. In these days of social unrest and world disequilibrium, many groups have been forced to examine their conventional roles, goals and relationships. The response of some has been to press towards a radical restructuring of society, including education. Others have sought to turn back to the past which, when viewed in retrospect, has a tendency to look so much better than it actually was. Most have sought to exercise some control over practices and events.

Public education is largely controlled by people outside the teaching profession who usually see it as serving two functions: 1) a social function – that is, passing on the local culture and engaging in social reform; and 2) an educational function – that is, teaching literacy, numeracy, scientific, humanistic, and vocational skills. But perhaps the strongest factor in the control of public education is that it is paid for by public money. It would be unrealistic to expect the tax-paying public to hand over control of an institution as important to the survival and well-being of society as education solely to educators whose aims, while laudable, may be running counter to prevailing trends and values. As ideologies rise and fall, so do societies' notions of what constitutes their well-being. Hence, while educators can influence to some degree the content of what is taught and the method by which it is taught, it is the public, through its elected or appointed officials, that ultimately determines the purpose and direction of education, and while this assumption may be challenged the practice is likely to continue.

Policy-making is an ongoing process. New policies arise out of current issues; new issues arise out of current policies. Controversy is always present as individuals and groups clash over values, priorities, and strategies. But policies provide some stability. Employees of an institution know what they *must* do, what they *may* do, and what they *must not* do. Traditions also provide some stability, but unlike policies, which are deliberately developed, traditions evolve over the years and tend to be accepted without question. Traditions can have both negative and positive effects on language teaching: they can impede change when teachers insist on clinging to past practices in the face of new knowledge and new circumstances; they can influence the nature and direction of change when teachers use traditional practices as guidelines for future action. Whether control is exercised through policies or traditions, it is a part of every language teacher's life.

The first section of this chapter (3.2) will look at the influence of local community groups on language teaching. This will be followed (3.3) by an examination of the various characteristics of students, teachers, curriculum and programs over which teachers may have total, some or no control. Then, because possession of information is the key to exercising control, the next section (3.4) will describe how teachers can become informed professionally. The concluding section (3.5) will investigate ways in which teachers can get community support for their programs.

3.2   The influence of local community groups

The attitudes, expectations and aspirations of individuals and the groups to which they belong play a large part in determining the future and fate of education and therefore of language teaching. When a cause is seen as a matter of mutual concern by a number of groups, their cooperation can result in a strong and powerful movement. But when the interests of one group negatively affect the interests of another group, unless a solution is quickly found, infighting can occur which benefits neither side and creates prolonged confusion for education. Language teachers are not only members of professional communities, but also of geo-political and common interest communities. They have therefore both the right and the opportunity to help various groups to frame their objectives and to carry them out in ways that will further the well-being of students and the various communities.

We will now examine ten groups at the local community level, that is, below the national level, and consider what influence they can have on language teaching.

Geo-political groups

NEIGHBORHOODS

The most significant factor in neighborhoods is their socio-economic make-up. In spite of attempts to mix people from high and low socio-economic groups through housing programs, most neighborhoods consist of people of roughly similar socio-economic status. High and low socio-economic status is caused by the unequal distribution of wealth among people. It is reflected in where and how people live and in their occupations, and tends to be passed on from generation to generation. Children are socialized not into the culture as a whole, but into sub-cultures as represented by high and low socio-economic status. They learn the values and customs of their sub-culture, and its expectations become their expectations. The socialization children undergo in their early years limits or increases their ability to function in the larger society, and particularly to take advantage of educational opportunities.

It has been proved time and time again that the socio-economic class children are born into is a determining factor in the progress they will make in school which in turn determines who will get to university.[1] A child with a high IQ from a low socio-economic class has less chance of reaching university than a child with a lower IQ from a high socio-economic class. Students entering the professions more often than not have professionals as parents. The reasons for this inequality of representation in post-secondary education are not hard to find.

One effect of low socio-economic status on children can be seen in the kinds of language skills they bring to school. Children from high socio-economic groups usually have well-developed language and thinking skills similar to those used by teachers in the classroom, such as questioning, answering, describing, predicting and conceptualizing. These children are accustomed to exploring an ever-widening world and to discussing their findings with adults. Children from low socio-economic groups, on the other hand, may have lived in a physically more restricted world where language is used primarily for the conduct of day-to-day affairs rather than for the clarification and expansion of concepts or the resolution of more distant and abstract problems. As language skills are transferable across languages, the kind of language skills children acquire in their first language may well affect their progress in mastering a second language. In addition the quality of life varies between high and low socio-economic groups. Children of the working poor have less nourishing diets and more sickness than their better-off peers. They live in more crowded conditions with little of the privacy they need for study or for sleep. The result is they are tired and apathetic while other children are energetic and enthusiastic. Wealthier parents can afford to give their children separate rooms and to support them financially during school and college. Children of the poor drop out of school into the labor force in order to assist their impoverished families or they leave home.

All this sets up different kinds of expectations in the children, their parents and their teachers. Children from the high socio-economic group grow up with the expectation that they will finish secondary school and take post-secondary training, an expectation which is reinforced by their parents and teachers. Few children from the low socio-economic group have the same expectations; most of them finish up in the non-academic stream where both parents and teachers feel they belong. Research has shown that the expectations parents and teachers have for children is a determining factor in the progress they make in school and in their choice of vocation.[2] Expectations can therefore decide which students will be studying modern languages in the senior grades and which will have dropped out by then.

Some minority groups occupy low socio-economic positions; consequently their children often have special educational needs. In order to address those needs adequately, teachers must know the historical and cultural backgrounds of the minority groups as well as the socio-economic factors which are holding the children back. An alternative educational program must take linguistic, cultural and economic factors into account if it is to serve the children well. Unfortunately, in the past some compensatory programs lasted for no more than one or two years. This was equivalent to providing malnourished children with a rich diet for a year and then returning them to their former inadequate rations. Any benefit was quickly eroded.

Adult members of minority groups who are part of the working poor may be disadvantaged because they do not have good control of the language of the workplace without which they cannot move from low-paying unskilled jobs to higher-paying skilled jobs. But unless language classes are provided free they may not be able to afford the fees. In any case, at the end of the day's work they may be too tired to concentrate on the intricacies of language learning.

Socio-economic status therefore affects 1) who will attend language-teaching classes, 2) how well they progress, and 3) their expectations for achievement. Teachers can assist their students by 1) addressing the specific needs of the students in their classes, 2) encouraging the institutions to mount programs which address their needs, and 3) supporting social and political actions which reduce gross economic inequalities among groups. In this regard, the community school movement of the last two decades has encouraged some neighborhoods to play a more influential role in education through the exercise of greater control over their local school by assuming some portion of the decision-making responsibilities that formerly belonged to professionals or politicians.

In many parts of the world, policies affecting public/state schools and junior colleges are established by elected representatives of the general public called 'members' or 'trustees' of a particular school or college board or local education authority. As they are not usually paid for their services, their motives for seeking office are not for financial gain. Some disapprove of the way schools are run and seek to improve them. Some feel they have a duty to run or are interested in getting some experience in a low level of politics before moving to a higher level. Some believe that a particular group should be represented. Once they have been elected they face the question: who are their constituents? Parents? Taxpayers? A specific group? A political party? Obviously at times these groups will be in conflict. What parents want for their children may be more than taxpayers are prepared to pay. What a minority group wants for its children may not be acceptable to the majority. These elected lay-educators have the responsibility of trying to reconcile multiple and diverse demands from various sectors of the electorate. In addition, they must bridge the gap between what the community demands and what professionals – teachers and administrators – see as educationally desirable and feasible.

School or college boards or councils are engaged in educational politics which will influence the quality of the institutions under their control. It is their responsibility to establish policies which will govern the operation of their institution(s) and which will be implemented by senior administrators and their staffs. Boards or councils must deal with two types of issues: those which are centered directly on specific institutions and deal with such matters as local programs and curricula, textbooks, and renovations; and those which are public issues such as the budget, taxes, teachers' salaries, and declining enrolment, and which therefore have a much wider appeal. Language-teaching issues may fall into either category. The choice of a particular school for the mounting of a new language program or the curriculum for the program are narrow issues and tend to involve only those immediately affected. But decisions to permit another language as the medium of instruction or to teach heritage languages in the schools often bring a much wider public into the fray.

The public has always felt it should have a voice in educational policy-making, perhaps because everyone has been through the educational process and therefore people think they know what they are talking about; perhaps because it is their money and their children that are at stake; or perhaps because a commitment to democratic principles requires people to assume some responsibility for policy-making in public institutions. Whatever the reasons, education is one place where a community and its official institutions can draw closer together through public input. School boards can involve the public in various ways. The lowest form of involvement consists of simply keeping people informed. Meaningful participation can, however, be kept to a minimum if people are not given sufficient information on which to make decisions or are not told where they can find it. At the next level, people are given an opportunity to make their opinions known through surveys or consultations but are excluded from the decision-making process. At a higher level, individuals are invited to join committees or task forces to make recommendations to the board, or groups are asked to submit briefs.

It is important to recognize the difference between community control and community participation:

> Under community control, the community negotiates politically to become entrusted with *all or most* decision-making responsibilities. Viable community participation, however, is that in which citizens and social agencies affected by schools *are partners* in making important school policy decisions in areas such as budget, curriculum planning, selection of school personnel, and plans for racial integration.[3]

Making provision for community participation, a necessary prelude to control, is one thing; getting people there is another. One is reminded of the interchange in Shakespeare's *Henry IV* when Glendower boasts, 'I can call spirits from the vasty deep.' To which Hotspur retorts, 'Why, so can I, or so can any man; But will they come when you do call for them?'

To arrive at policy decisions, boards usually identify the problem, gather facts, consider various solutions and their possible implications and consequences and select the one which will help them to attain their stated goal. School boards, however, do not exist in isolation from other political systems in the community. They must interact with and be responsive to those who deal with zoning, health, parks, population control, housing, energy, and the environment, as well as with the senior levels of government. Often boards must compromise between the various demands, given that funds are not exhaustive. They come under pressure from left-wing and right-wing groups, and from special interest groups, including teachers. If the public changes its mind between elections and votes in a new slate of officers, education can undergo a dramatic change of direction. New theories and practices in education, when adopted by a board, can produce alternate schools, open-area schools, value schools and other programs, which are cut once the pendulum swings the other way.

Board decisions may affect the following aspects of language teachers' work:
- the language which is to be used as the medium of instruction and the languages which are to be taught as subjects;
- the status of their programs and consequently the status of language teachers;
- the goals and design of the program;
- the funding of the program;
- material and human resources.

School or college board decisions regarding language programs may be an indication of the public's attitude towards specific languages and cultures, and may reflect, at times, a strong ethno-centrism. Teachers' representatives can, however, usually meet with the board to present the professional point-of-view, but it is encumbent on them to be well-informed on their topic, a matter which will be taken up later on in this chapter.

Common interest groups

THE FAMILY

Through their families children acquire a particular status in the community which, as we saw earlier, affects the way in which the community and the school will treat them. Children are also affected by their own family's organization: child-centered or adult-centered; nuclear or extended; single parent or two parents. The family leaves its imprint on its members in various ways which affect their performance in language-teaching classrooms.

The intellectual and emotional development of children begins in the home, and their value systems are shaped there. In particular they acquire a specific learning style which they take to school. They may, for example, learn new concepts largely through asking or answering questions or they may learn them by observing and experimenting. That is, for some children knowledge is acquired primarily through language, whereas for others knowledge is acquired primarily through action. While this may seem simplistic as obviously all children use language and all children are active, the degree of emphasis placed on different modes of learning within the home establishes the children's expectations of how they will learn in school. But just as children have their different learning styles, so teachers have their different teaching styles. When children are placed in classrooms where the teaching style does not mesh with their learning style, the resultant discord will frustrate both teachers and children, no matter what the subject area. Learning styles are an integral part of child-rearing systems and are affected by socio-economic status as well as by cultural mores and practices.

The degree of security and support provided by families to students can affect their progress. Children's sense of security can be adversely affected by marriage breakdown, by migration from rural to urban living or from one country to another, and by clashes between their family's value system and that of the dominant society. These feelings of insecurity can be offset when families encourage students to continue their education and to set their goals high, and further when they ensure that the necessary financial support will be there for as long as they need it. Adequate financial support is, of course, particularly important to adult students, who, having immigrated to a new land or gone abroad to study, must master the new language if they are to become participating members of the social, educational, vocational or political life of the community. Without sufficient financial support students may not be able to attend class regularly or to give their full attention to their studies.

Parents' expectations of the degree of control they may exercise over their children's education varies from culture to culture. Some parents are content to leave it to the school to make major decisions over what their children will learn and in what programs or streams their children will be placed. Other parents believe it is their right and duty to make such decisions, with the result that control of language programs may be exercised by families in association with teachers through organizations such as parent–teacher or home–school associations or parent consultative committees.

Families which are members of minority ethnic groups play an important role in the maintenance of ancestral or heritage languages. Where there is a strong attachment to the ancestral language, children will grow up speaking that language, as well as the language of the dominant majority, and may be required by their parents to attend an ethnic language school after regular school. Where, however, the attachment to the ancestral language and pride in the culture is less strong, the children may grow up resisting the culture and resenting any hours spent in the heritage language classroom. The extent of the family or group's devotion to its language and culture is also reflected in the pressure it puts on schools to mount heritage language programs. The acquisition of the dominant language by children, when it is not known by the parents, can affect the cohesion and therefore the stability of the family as the older and younger generations find it more and more difficult to communicate and to understand each other's point-of-view, and so the old traditional roles change.

Families affect children's intellectual and emotional development, their learning styles, their expectations of what schools and therefore language programs can do for them, their sense of security, and their attitude towards their heritage language where this applies. Language teachers can assist their students by 1) becoming familiar with their different learning styles and adapting their teaching styles to accommodate them, at least initially, so as to prevent friction; 2) working with parents to help them understand the goals of the second language program and how these will assist their children; 3) raising their own expectations of what their students can achieve; 4) encouraging both parents and the community to provide students with moral and financial support; and 5) supporting parent–teacher organizations.

SPEECH COMMUNITIES

Speech communities not only share a common language or dialect, they also share certain values and attitudes regarding language form and language use. Although English is spoken throughout Britain, there are various different speech communities identifiable through dialectal differences and through the attitudes the members hold towards speakers of other dialects. Professor Higgins in *My Fair Lady* gives expression to one attitude when he says, 'An Englishman's way of speaking absolutely classifies him. The moment he talks he makes some other Englishman despise him.' In the United States there are large pockets of non-English-speaking people who constitute separate speech communities based on a language such as Spanish. However, not all speakers of Spanish in the United States are members of the same speech community despite their common language. Mexicans, Cubans and Puerto Ricans form separate speech communities because of their distinct histories and differing attitudes and values. Speech communities such as those found in Indian reservations or ghettos may have clearly defined geographical boundaries, but for others the edges are diffused where two languages or dialects intermingle.

Speech communities can act as comfortable and perhaps necessary havens where members can maintain an identity separate from that of the mainstream society. Individuals may wish to preserve a particular speech style in order to be recognized as a member of a particular speech community to which they have a strong loyalty rather than adopting the speech style of the majority and joining what may be the prestige community, and this is, of course, their right.

Some speech communities are socially disadvantaged and/or stigmatized. Attempts have been made through various early intervention programs to lessen the language disadvantages that some small children face on entering school. But while lack of fluency in the language of instruction may be one problem facing the children, their greater and more lasting disadvantage, economic insecurity, lies with the unequal distribution of wealth in society and the unequal access by adults to employment and to other economic opportunities, caused, in some instances, by prejudice on the part of others. Remedies must therefore be sought in the root causes of the speech community's difficulties; remedies cannot address language alone as if that were sufficient to restore the balance. Too often compensatory programs have only a short-term effect, having their base in what bureaucrats think will be good for the community rather than in what the community is seeking for itself. Language teaching can certainly help speech communities to preserve their identities while participating in the life of the mainstream community, but language teaching alone will not redress economic imbalance. Teachers can help by 1) recognizing the various speech communities from which their students are drawn, 2) understanding both the goals and the concerns of each speech community, and 3) permitting the members of the speech community to have some say in the process of education as it affects them.

MINORITY GROUPS

The term 'minority group' refers here to clusters of people who speak among themselves a non-official language or a language not spoken by the dominant group in the community. In addition, the minority group will probably follow certain practices or hold to certain values different from those of the dominant group. Michael Novak describes an ethnic group as follows:

> What is an ethnic group? It is a group with historical memory, real or imaginary. One belongs to an ethnic group in part involuntarily, in part by choice. Given a grandparent or two, one chooses to shape one's consciousness by one history rather than another. Ethnic memory is not a set of events remembered, but rather a set of instincts, feelings, intimacies, expectations, patterns of emotion and behavior; a sense of reality; a set of stories for individuals – and for the people as a whole – to live out.[4]

Minority groups usually have two concerns for the younger generation: 1) that they will continue to preserve their heritage language and customs; and 2) that they will have access to the social, political, and vocational systems of the dominant group.

According to John Friesen, schooling can be used in five different ways, each one of which affects negatively or positively the preservation of the language and culture of minority groups:

A. *Schooling as assimilation.* The pupose behind schooling as assimilation is to make children of minority groups think, speak and act like majority group children. The educational policies of colonizing nations were often assimilationist. Children were schooled in the language of the colonizing power and were often not allowed to speak their own language. This resulted in the death or near death of many languages and the loss of cultural practices.

B. *Schooling as a cultural wedge.* Schooling has the capacity to drive a wedge between children and their heritage culture and language and between the minority group and the majority group. This can occur when the values taught in school are in conflict with the values taught at home. Alienation builds between the child and the home and the school. When the children lose fluency in the home language and when the school cannot talk to parents in their language, the cultural wedge divides the community.

C. *Schooling as cultural isolation.* Schooling can be used to isolate minority-group children from majority-group children. A minority group determined to keep its language and culture and perhaps its religion may steadfastly refuse to send its children to the local school but may educate them in isolation using the language of the minority as the medium. As the children grow up they may find it increasingly difficult to mix with people of the dominant group whose culture and language are foreign to them.

D. *Schooling as a synthesizing factor.* Schooling can be used to synthesize and harmonize the cultural and religious goals of a minority group. Schooling is seen as an extension of the family or religious life of a particular sect. Unlike public/state schools which cater to a very broad section of children, schools which accept only the children of one group do not have to be tolerant and accepting of different viewpoints. Children in separate schools are usually expected to study their ancestral language (the language of the home and the religion) and the language of the dominant society.

E. *Schooling and cultural preservation.* Schooling can be used to preserve a minority culture and its language while permitting children to become thoroughly absorbed in the majority culture. Children attend the regular public/state school during the day and an ethnic language school during the evening or weekends where they study the ancestral language and culture.[5]

In many parts of the world there has been a rising interest in the transmission and preservation of minority languages and cultures. The concept of cultural pluralism or multiculturalism is being tested and examined in countries having diverse populations as communities work out what degree of difference between groups is acceptable and what this difference will be. A former United States Commissioner of Education, James E. Allen, Jr, wrote:

> The day of the melting pot is over. No longer is it the ideal of each minority to become an indistinguishable part of the majority.

Today, each strives to maintain its identity while seeking its rightful share of the social, economic, and political fruits of our system. Self-help and self-determination have become the rallying cries of all minorities.[6]

Already the effects of the new movement have been felt in language teaching:

1. Strong attempts are being made to revive and maintain indigenous languages. Linguists and second language teachers are working with native people to help them describe their language, produce a written form if necessary, prepare teaching materials, and train native language teachers.
2. Immigrant minority groups are seeking to improve the quality of teaching in their heritage or ancestral language schools through better teaching methods and better trained teachers.
3. In regions where the minority group constitutes a significant percentage of the population, minority-group leaders are asking that their language be taught in the schools as a second language and that it be used in some subject areas as the medium of instruction. Bilingual–bicultural education is now practiced in a number of countries.
4. Since the publication of *Learning To Be* in 1972 by Unesco, increasing attention has been paid to the language needs of young children just starting school whose higher education will be in a second language. Teaching children in their vernacular for the first three years of school while adding the second language is widely recommended and is common practice in some parts of the world. But where numbers do not permit this to occur or policies prohibit it, small children have to make the difficult adjustment from the home language to the language of the school on entry.

While minority groups are concerned about the preservation of their heritage language and culture, they are also concerned that through an appropriate education their young people will have access to all the vocations and professions and will participate in the social, economic and political life of the community. The term 'equal opportunity' when applied to education resulted a few years ago in various kinds of 'Headstart' programs where the emphasis was on trying to place all children on the same starting line when they entered school. But it has not worked well enough, for when outcomes are examined, the children of some minorities are not proportionally represented in school-leaving classes or within post-secondary institutions. Minority groups are increasingly demanding educational programs that will help them to keep their distinct identity while opening the doors to the opportunities found in the dominant culture. Teachers knowledgeable about the advantages and disadvantages of different kinds of language-teaching programs can assist communities in arriving at the right policy for different groups.

RELIGIOUS GROUPS

Because religion is a powerful force in the lives of some people, they have been willing to take whatever steps are necessary either to maintain their religion in the face of opposition, or to bring others to their way of thinking. The faith they follow is expressed through language, through the ritual of prayer, through songs, hymns, and psalms, and through the well-known phrases of the scriptures, so that those who profess the faith are emotionally tied to the language of their faith. This linking of religion and language has resulted in the demise of some languages and the maintenance of others. Hence religious groups have had both positive and negative effects on the teaching of foreign or second languages and on the maintenance of heritage languages.

The loss or weakening of some native Indian languages and cultures in North America can be ascribed to some degree to missionaries who insisted on expounding the scriptures in the language in which they felt most comfortable – their own. They were backed up by governments which established an 'English only' policy believing that only by losing their native tongues and mastering English would Indian people be able to compete with the white man. The policy was clearly assimilationist and was to remain in effect until after the Second World War. For years the education of native Indian children was carried on in the language of the proselytizing church, sometimes in day schools on the reserve, sometimes in residential schools off the reserve. The children and grandchildren of the first converts steadily lost touch with the language and culture of their forebears and were unable to communicate with their elders. They were taught, directly and indirectly, that their ancestral language and culture were of little worth compared to that of the white community. But, in addition, the second language was often poorly taught by untrained teachers so that the children became neither fluent nor literate in either language. During the last two decades native people have been given more control over their children's education and some bands are now using their language as the medium of instruction or teaching it as a subject along with its cultural attributes, but for other bands the language is virtually dead. What has happened in North America has happened elsewhere in the world where the colonizing power has permitted religious groups to proselytize through the schools in a foreign language. More recently, however, missionaries with training in linguistics have provided a written form for many previously unwritten languages thereby strengthening them, as well as requiring the training of native language teachers.

Some immigrant groups, particularly those which were persecuted for their beliefs in their homelands, have tried to preserve their religion and the language in which it is encoded. In North America religious sects, such as the Amish and Hutterite people, have isolated themselves from the mainstream culture and have built and staffed their own schools where the group's values are taught through the group's language. On the other hand, some ethnic groups, such as the Ukrainians, have succeeded in mixing with the mainstream culture while maintaining their religion and, to a considerable degree, their culture and language, a remarkable feat for a group that has received few new immigrants to bolster it since the first settlers arrived during the early part of the century.

In some parts of the world the education system was set up along religious lines, for example, one system for Protestants and another for Roman Catholics. In the province of Quebec, Canada, where the greater proportion of the French settlers tended to be Roman Catholics and the English Protestants, the division also fell along language lines. The French-speaking children enrolled in the Catholic school system and the English-speaking children in the Protestant school system, thus helping to create the 'two solitudes', two speech communities who lived apart while inhabiting the same geographic area. However, the separation of schools by faith and language enabled the French Canadians to hold onto their linguistic and cultural heritage for over two centuries.

Teachers working with students from distinct religious groups must be sensitive to the group's history and beliefs, recognizing that the group's future is rooted in its past and helped or hindered by the present.

PRESSURE GROUPS

Pressure groups provide a channel through which concerns can be expressed and demands made. Their aim is to affect policy formation and policy implementation. Pressure groups may be ad hoc collections of individuals brought together for one purpose or they may be duly constituted organizations; they may be local or national in scope. While changes to society can be enforced from the top down by government decree, pressure groups believe changes can also be initiated from the bottom up through placing pressure on those in authority. Increasingly politicians have had to listen to the demands of those who would make changes within the educational system. Indeed, pressure groups are an integral part of the process of educational governance and cannot be ignored.

The community as control

Pressure groups serve three functions:
- they bring together people with similar concerns and convictions, or people who are in similar circumstances;
- they delineate the issues and provide information to the authorities and the public;
- they bring pressure to bear on decision-making bodies using a variety of strategies.

The degree of effectiveness of a pressure group will depend on a number of factors:
1. its ability to influence those in power over a sustained period of time;
2. the support it can gain for its cause from other people and groups in the community;
3. the legitimacy of its concern and of its proposed solution;
4. the depth of its knowledge concerning all facets of its cause and therefore its ability to respond confidently to questions;
5. the number of other pressure groups who are simultaneously trying to get attention and whose causes may detract from its own;
6. the acceptability and appropriateness of the means used by the group to promote its cause: petitions, the use of the media, electing members to public office, demonstrations, and meeting with officials may all have their place at different times during negotiations.

Professional communities

EDUCATIONAL INSTITUTIONS

Local educational institutions, whether catering to children or adults, have varying degrees of autonomy. In some countries all authority is centralized in a national ministry of education which regulates all aspects of the system, including curriculum, admission, attendance, graduation of students, and certification of teachers. In other countries all decisions are made by locally elected or appointed councils: curriculum is designed locally; admission and graduation requirements are set locally, and teachers need only meet local hiring requirements. Often authority is split, with the ministry of education issuing broad directives within which local authorities have some leeway to mount programs which are responsive to local needs. In such cases it is imperative that language teachers know which group has decision-making powers over the items listed below, so that they know who to approach when the need arises:
- the goals of the language program;
- funding for the implementation and maintenance of the program;
- the curriculum;

- the provision of textbooks, audio-visual equipment and materials, and support staff;
- the design of the program including class size, admission requirements, meeting times, length of the program, student fees;
- the hiring and firing of teachers;
- the evaluation of the administration of the program, of the quality of teaching, and of the outcomes.

The term *bureaucracy* has taken on pejorative connotations. Theoretically, bureaucracies are supposed to heighten efficiency and to reduce friction and costs. However, they have come under increased criticism as being wasteful, unwieldy, impersonal, and unable to respond quickly to local needs. Undoubtedly, the organizational structure imposes constraints on policy-making and policy-implementation, but it is likely that established policies, by imposing constraints on the organizational structure, also inhibit action. The larger an institution or an educational system grows, the more centralized it will probably become. While decentralization has some advantages – people closer to the students can make faster and better decisions in response to their needs than can those far removed; it has some disadvantages – duplication of effort, lack of uniformity, failure to tap the advice of specialists. But whatever the power structure, language teachers have to work within it and to use it for the benefit of their students. With computers capable of taking over much of the detailed work of administration, there may be more time for administrators and language teachers to explore various facets of language teaching and learning and to make decisions which increasingly take into account both the needs of individuals and the changes taking place in world trade, technology and communication.

The status of language teachers within educational institutions can vary according to what language they teach to whom. Teaching a European language to academic-stream students was for many years seen as an occupation of higher prestige than teaching the official language to immigrants, and this was often reflected in different pay scales. In recent years the teaching of English as a second or foreign language has enjoyed increasing popularity. However, the prestige accorded the teaching of any language in an institution still depends on the time and funding allotted to it by senior administrators, and the morale of language teachers depends on the atmosphere which is created by these decisions.

TEACHER-TRAINING INSTITUTIONS

Around the world, teachers are accorded varying degrees of status ranging from very high to very low, and this is often reflected in the financial and moral support given to the local teacher-training institution.

The community as control

In some parts of the world, teachers of 5–12-year-olds are made out of those students who have failed to gain a place at university. At best, they may receive a one- or two-year training course which may or may not include work in second language teaching, and, apart from some short inservice work, this minimal training is (quite wrongly) considered adequate for the education of elementary children. In other parts of the world, a university degree at the Bachelor's or Master's level is required before a teaching certificate is granted, perhaps with a specialty in a particular field such as language teaching.

Good classroom teaching depends on good teacher-training which in turn depends on good research in the theory and practice of first and second language teaching-learning and in related disciplines such as linguistics, sociolinguistics, psycholinguistics, anthropology, sociology and communications. Hence teacher-training colleges which are isolated from universities where research is normally carried on are sometimes in danger of becoming inbred and out-of-date.

Teacher-training institutions have to prepare language teachers to work with both children and adults at the beginning, intermediate and advanced levels and to provide them with information, theory and practice. In addition, in some parts of the world they must retrain teachers to work in multicultural classrooms which are replacing the monocultural classrooms in which they originally trained. The availability of training programs for prospective language teachers and the quality of those programs depend on the depth of the commitment of the decision-makers to provide the necessary funds and support. The quality also depends on the willingness of the teaching profession to provide opportunities for student-teachers to practice the required skills in their classrooms under the supervision of trained and experienced teachers.

In 1972 TESOL (Teachers of English to Speakers of Other Languages) published some guidelines on the preparation and certification of teachers of English as a second or foreign language. The statement set out the role of the teacher, the desirable personal qualities, professional competencies and experience, along with suggested objectives and features of a teacher-preparation program. This action, coupled with a demand from the field for better-trained teachers, increased both the quantity of training programs for ESL teachers and their quality. As more and more teachers in the various areas of language teaching began to hold a body of specialized knowledge in common they were able to view themselves as an emerging professional group with the rights and responsibilities that that implies, and therefore to exercise greater control over their individual and collective destinies.

ORGANIZATIONS

Teachers have always had one kind of power – the power to influence and perhaps change the lives of their students – but that is not the same as the power to control their own professional lives. As John Martin Rich says: 'Teachers who have little opportunity to utilize their full range of ability and to continue to grow as professional persons because of the bureaucratic structure and the types of controls to which they are subject, are unlikely to develop their professional qualities.'[7] One way to gain power is by banding together.

During recent years, language teachers have established local, national and international organizations. Some consist entirely of teachers working in specific programs such as bilingual education or second language teaching; others embrace teachers from different programs. These organizations may, through their constitutions, decide to play different roles and perform different functions:
- they may act as advocates for teachers, seeking increases in salaries and improved working conditions for their members;
- they may act as advocates for students, seeking improved language-learning conditions and increased availability of programs;
- they may work closely with teacher-training institutions in the planning and implementing of preservice programs for language teachers;
- they may offer inservice training courses for their members;
- they may engage in in-class research into methods and techniques;
- they may research and report on the state of language teaching in their region;
- they may disperse information to their members through newsletters and journals;
- they may work cooperatively with other organizations for a cause which is of mutual interest.

The ability of organizations to help teachers and students depends upon governments allowing such organizations to exist, on adequate funding, on a strong but empathetic leadership, on the readiness of members to give their time and energy, and on the opportunities that members have to exchange ideas and to provide mutual support.

Language teachers have formed their own organizations, some of which are international in scope. These organizations hold annual conventions where recent research is presented and discussed alongside practical 'hands-on' workshops. Special interest groups within the organizations address the concerns of elementary, secondary and post-secondary teachers, and national and international issues, such as the right of children to begin their education in their mother tongue, and various other socio-political matters. From time to time an organization will present a brief to government on a topic it feels strongly about and will lobby politicians.

Parents' groups such as the parent–teacher association or home–school association and ethnic societies can also influence language teaching. These groups can be powerful forces for the improvement of education, not simply by raising funds for equipment but by lobbying for better programs for minority-group children and for greater opportunities for all children to learn a second language.

In the adult field, there are many organizations with concern for specific groups of clients, such as the undereducated, the new immigrant, and the foreign student. In each case, language may be part of the adjustment the students are trying to make to their situation. Coordination and cooperation among educationally-related organizations has resulted in progress on behalf of both teachers and their students. (See Appendix C for a short list of national and international organizations.)

3.3 Characteristics of students, teachers, curriculum and programs

Control over language teaching lies with those who have the power to decide *who* will teach *which language* to *whom*, *when*, *where*, and for *how long*. All power may be concentrated in one person or it may be divided between several people at different levels of the decision-making hierarchy.

Provided their ideas and practices do not run counter to the goals and values of society, teachers and administrators are usually in control of the organization of classes and methods of instruction once the broader issues have been resolved. However, as no two classrooms and no two communities are identical, the degree of control that individual teachers can exercise over their teaching situations varies considerably.

The three major components in any language-teaching classroom are students, teachers, and curriculum and program. These can be viewed as a triangle with constant ongoing interactions between the parts:

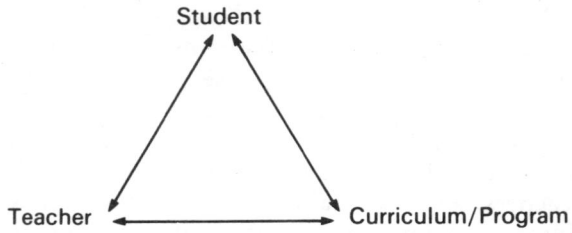

Each of these components can be broken down into greater detail. For example, students have different educational backgrounds, come from different socio-economic groups, and have different reasons for wanting or not wanting to learn another language. Teachers have varying degrees of control over the details which make up the characteristics of the three components; that is, teachers may have no control over students' socio-economic status, some control over their own working conditions, and total control over the choice of textbooks. It is incumbent upon teachers to be aware of those areas over which they can exercise control and those areas where control lies with others who may or may not be influenced by the advice of teachers. The remainder of this section will be devoted to an examination of the diverse characteristics of the classroom over which teachers have differing degrees of control.

Characteristics of students

To learn is to change. The process of education within the classroom has, therefore, the power to change the learner. Teachers can exert a direct influence on their students through face-to-face encounters in the classroom or an indirect influence through their involvement in issues affecting their students' lives beyond the classroom. Certain student characteristics can be changed for the better, some can be exploited for the students' advantage, some can be strengthened, but all must be taken into account, remembering that students are more than the sum of their characteristics.

Each characteristic below should be considered in terms of its past, its present and its future contribution to the well-being of the individual student and the individual class, and in terms of the degree and kind of control the teacher has over the management of the characteristic for the benefit of the student(s) both within the classroom and outside it.

The following example, using the first item in the list below, may make this clear:

> *Students' attitudes towards learning the target language*
> A particular student holds a very negative attitude towards the target language and has persuaded some of his classmates to adopt his attitude. The teacher is working to change his attitude so that his future attitude and that of his classmates will be more positive. Success, however, may be slight as the students' parents hold very strong views against speakers of the target language. The teacher's control over the situation is therefore limited.

A teacher's control over each of the following characteristics will vary considerably from one classroom to another:
  1. students' attitudes towards learning the target language;
  2. their goals for learning the target language;

3. their fluctuating motivational levels;
4. their physical health;
5. their emotional stability;
6. their intellectual capacity and development;
7. their previous education;
8. the learning style they bring to the classroom;
9. the other languages they know;
10. their membership in the dominant or minority group;
11. their socio-economic status;
12. the moral and financial support they receive from their families to continue their education;
13. their perception of the career opportunities that learning the target language may open up.

Characteristics of teachers

The following excerpt directed towards schools can apply equally to adult institutions:

> No priority is more fundamental than the need to attract into the schools a steady stream of highly educated, gifted, knowledgeable, sensitive and dedicated teachers, and to give them full scope for using their knowledge and talents to the fullest in the interest of the children entrusted to them.[8]

The point is how much scope do teachers have to become highly educated, gifted, knowledgeable, sensitive and dedicated, and to use their knowledge and talents in the interest of their students? The answers will vary widely from institution to institution and from nation to nation.

The characteristics over which teachers may be able to exert some control can be subsumed under four headings:

KNOWLEDGE

Teachers must have indepth knowledge of their subject field and must keep up-to-date, that is, teaching and continuous learning are inseparable. In addition, they must have a broad education covering the sciences and the humanities. Language, after all, penetrates all of life. Teachers must understand the process of education as it affects their subject area and their students.

SKILLS

Good teaching results from competent classroom organization and management, from clear and stimulating lesson presentation, and from the effective use of a variety of techniques. These skills must be practiced and evaluated.

PERSONAL QUALITIES

While we do not know the precise mix of personal qualities which results in an effective teacher, some of the following appear to be essential: enthusiasm, kindness, humor, patience, sincerity, determination, intellectual curiosity, and respect for others.

PROFESSIONALISM

Although we often speak of the teaching *profession*, in fact it often appears to lie halfway between trade unionism on the one hand and full professionalism on the other; perhaps it would be fairer to describe it as an 'emerging profession'. Teachers bargain for working conditions and sometimes go out on strike similar to trade unions, but, like other professionals, they can influence, if not control, standards and can engage in activities and research that improve the quality of teaching and enhance the profession in the eyes of the public. The strength of the profession results from the sum of the attitudes and actions of individual teachers.

The following items are those over which language teachers can perhaps exercise some control:
1.   the nature and extent of their preservice training;
2.   their continuing inservice training;
3.   their competency to plan and organize for learning;
4.   the choice of role they assume in the classroom – director, facilitator, lecturer, co-learner, etc.;
5.   the effectiveness of their lesson preparation;
6.   those personal qualities which need to be further developed;
7.   the respect they draw from their colleagues and from the community;
8.   their working conditions;
9.   their attitude towards their job, employer, and profession;
10. their access to professional journals;
11. their active participation in a teachers' organization.

Characteristics of the curriculum and program

What is to be taught and the conditions under which it is to be taught constitute the curriculum and the program. As various administrative constraints may be placed on teachers, the degree of control they can exercise over the following items may be very diverse:
1.   the goals of the program;
2.   the theoretical model on which the curriculum is based;

3. the design of the curriculum;
4. the linguistic and cultural content;
5. the method used in the classroom (audio-lingual, cognitive-code, 'silent way', communicative approach etc.);
6. the techniques used in the classroom (drills, small-group work, field trips, etc.);
7. the degree of emphasis placed on each of the four skills of listening, speaking, reading and writing;
8. the availability and/or choice of print and non-print materials;
9. the adequacy of funding for the program;
10. the length of the program and the frequency with which the class meets;
11. the size of the class;
12. the range of ability levels and ages within the class;
13. the qualifications of the teaching staff.

3.4 Becoming informed professionally

The knowledge a language teacher must have in order to do a competent job in the classroom must include both theory and practice. While student-teachers are usually very concerned with practice, it is theory which provides the foundation on which their future development as professionals will be built. Jack Richards and Ted Rodgers suggest a three-tiered hierarchy joining theory and practice under the umbrella heading of Method which consists of Approach, Design, and Procedure. *Approach* encompasses both theories of language and theories of language learning. *Design* for language teaching includes 1) the content of instruction, 2) learner roles in the system, 3) teacher roles in the system, and 4) instructional materials, types and functions. *Procedure* focuses on techniques, practices and activities that operate in teaching and learning a language according to a particular method.[9]

There are six ways in which teachers can become informed professionally: 1) preservice training, 2) inservice training, 3) conferences, 4) newsletters and journals, 5) through committee work and 6) through discussion with colleagues.

Preservice training

Preservice training is training taken before a teacher obtains a teaching position. The length of the training and the subject matter studied vary from program to program, but will usually include work in both theory and practice, the latter often involving observation and practice teaching under the guidance of a qualified teacher. Teacher-training programs for language teachers may be given through colleges and universities, or government departments, or private agencies, or commercial language schools. The programs may, on successful completion, terminate in a certificate or diploma or degree.

Course or unit topics usually center around
- theories of first and second language acquisition
- linguistics
- sociolinguistics and psycholinguistics
- methods of teaching second languages
- classroom techniques and procedures
- testing and evaluation
- curriculum and syllabus design
- materials evaluation
- program planning
- observation and practice teaching

Students seeking entry to a training program should investigate the quality of the program before enrolling. This can be done by talking to practicing teachers and administrators, particularly those who have gone through the program or who hire graduates of the program. Prospective student-teachers should also determine whether the program will permit them at a later date to continue their studies at a different institution.

Inservice training

Even teachers who have completed their preservice training still have much to learn about language teaching. Indeed, most teachers continue to learn more about both the art and craft of teaching until the end of their careers. While some teachers may have both the desire and the opportunity to return to college or university to take a higher certificate or degree, many will acquire additional professional knowledge that will keep them up-to-date through inservice training.

Inservice training may occur through
- lectures by local or visiting experts
- demonstrations by practicing teachers or consultants
- displays of materials, print and non-print
- workshops

Workshops are usually popular if the format consists of a short presentation followed by a cooperative attempt to find practical solutions for the issue under discussion. Good workshops are well planned. They try to address the needs of teachers and to provide continuity and orderly development. They can be offered during or after working hours, but if the latter, they must take into account the fatigue that teachers may be suffering from after a day of teaching. It is debatable whether attendance should be voluntary or compulsory. An audience of interested volunteers is always a pleasure to instruct – they are there because they want to be there so motivation is high. But often it is those who do not attend who need the instruction, so a case can be made for compelling the unwilling to attend. Workshops may be mounted by an institution or a group of institutions, by government or private agencies, or by teachers and their professional organizations. To be effective they must be well planned, taking the following questions into account:

1. *Topics.* What topics need to be addressed? Who may suggest topics? How will they make them known and to whom?
2. *Workshop objectives.* What will be the main objective? What will the workshop achieve?
3. *Participants.* Who may participate?
4. *Time.* What day and hour will accommodate most people? How long will the workshop last?
5. *Presenter.* Who is the best qualified person to present the workshop?
6. *Size of group.* What is the optimum size of the group?
7. *Funding.* Who will pay whatever costs are incurred?
8. *Format.* What format will allow for presentation of important information and interaction between the participants and presenter through a 'hands-on' approach?
9. *Evaluation.* How will the process and the results of the workshop be evaluated?
10. *Follow-up.* What follow-up activities will be planned?

Conferences

Growing interest in language learning and teaching has resulted in an increase in the number of conferences related specifically to second language teaching and learning. Conferences are held at the local, national and international level. Readers should acquaint themselves with local and national conferences which are usually advertised in local and national journals and newsletters.

In addition, language teachers can learn much from associated disciplines and subject areas and should consider attending conferences dealing with some of the following topics: linguistics, sociolinguistics, psycholinguistics, ethnic studies, cultural pluralism or multiculturalism, teaching reading or written composition to first language speakers, and curriculum design. Conferences on home–school relations or immigrant or refugee settlement may also prove useful to some teachers.

Conferences enable participants 1) to meet people teaching in similar situations and to learn from them; 2) to see in the flesh people whose books and/or articles are well-known; 3) to be stimulated by the findings of research revealed in the sessions and by the flow of ideas;

4) to examine new print and non-print materials on view in the publishers' display area; and 5) to travel out of their own region, perhaps out of their own country.

Newsletters and journals

Newsletters and journals serve two different functions though each may, from time to time, encroach a little on the other. The function of the newsletter is to provide information of immediate and relevant concern to its readers on what has happened, is happening, and is likely to happen within the profession. Newsletters are put out by local, national and international organizations and are usually paid for through the members fees to the association. Journals, on the other hand, provide their readers with indepth articles covering the theory and practice of second language teaching, the findings of recent research, and book reviews. Journals are usually published by single interest groups and may be either refereed or non-refereed. A refereed journal has an editorial board of competent professionals which decides which articles will be accepted for publication and which rejected. Institutional and individual subscriptions are available to most journals. Language teachers should ensure they have regular access to at least one professional journal. (See Appendix A for a list of major journals.)

Committee work

Committee work can be professionally interesting and educational. It can provide an opportunity for language teachers to examine a particular issue in depth and so to become fully informed; to meet colleagues with similar concerns and to exchange ideas; to broaden their understanding of why things are the way they are and to explore acceptable methods of making change.

Professional committees deal with a wide range of issues such as the following:
– working conditions
– salaries and benefits
– ethical issues
– program and curriculum planning
– evaluation of teachers and programs
– preservice and inservice training
After a few years of teaching, many language teachers develop a special area of interest which they pursue, perhaps through committee work with interested colleagues. The profession needs both the generalist and the specialist who examine what the other is doing and inform each other of the latest developments in their own fields thus creating a healthy state of tension and dynamism.

Discussion with colleagues

All the preceding items have dealt with formal ways in which language teachers can become professionally knowledgeable. There is one informal way which is as old as teaching; that is, through colleague talking to colleague. Experienced teachers have a responsibility to explore ideas with those around them, and to pass on their wisdom to new teachers. No new teacher should be left without a mentor.

3.5 Getting support for your program

Good programs don't just happen – they are carefully planned. The first step in the process is to establish a need for a particular language-teaching program. Next, the objectives must be set and a program designed. As the program must have the support of the institutional community and the local community if it is to obtain resources and attract students, good public relations strategies must form part of the plan. Finally, the program must be evaluated and the findings reported back to all interested parties in the community.

Recognizing a need for a program

As most language programs are initiated and run by educational institutions, it is up to administrators and teachers to keep their ears close to the ground for any hints of unmet needs within the community. There are a number of indicators they can watch for:

1. *Briefs.* Groups within the community who feel their language needs are not being met may submit briefs to their local or national governments requesting action. These briefs will probably be available to local institutions and make a focal point for dialogue.
2. *Task forces.* Task forces established to look into a particular social issue such as school dropouts, unemployment within a specific group or the resettlement of immigrants may include recommendations for language classes.
3. *Nation-wide tests.* Nation-wide tests may indicate the need to establish or improve on language-teaching programs. They may, for example, demonstrate a need for better services to people who do not speak the official language with the same fluency as their mother-tongue peers, or they may suggest that modern language teaching should begin in the early grades.
4. *Reports (research and descriptive).* Sometimes through a research report or a descriptive report of a program mounted elsewhere, a previously unrecognized need is brought into prominence. Research

into immersion programs calmed the fears of some parents that using two languages in school would retard their children, and the demand for immersion programs grew. Descriptions of English in the workplace programs encouraged others to try this method of upgrading their workers' language facility.

5. *Community agencies.* Social workers, counsellors and others who work in government or private community agencies can often detect a need for special language training for a particular group of their clients who seem to be linguistically disadvantaged. Constant liaison should be maintained with community workers so that needs can be identified early before the crisis stage is reached.

6. *Schools.* Schools are particularly well-placed to determine which children and their families are handicapped in their educational, vocational or social lives because of lack of oral fluency or literacy in a specific language. A system of multicultural or bilingual home–school workers speeds up identification of learning problems.

7. *Employers.* Employers of skilled, semi-skilled or unskilled labor know whether a low-level language ability is causing some employees to remain in low-paying jobs and others to constitute a safety hazard because they do not understand instructions. They may be interested in upgrading their employees' language skills if they are familiar with language for specific purpose programs, such as those which take place on the work site.

8. *Official statistics.* Official statistics can sometimes give forewarning of a developing trend within the population that may result in the near or distant future in an unmet need if steps are not taken soon to develop the right kind of program. For example, an increase in any of the following areas should be a cause of concern for language program planners: 1) the number of non-official language speakers entering the country; or 2) the rate of unemployment among speakers of a particular minority language; or 3) the number of children entering school from homes where the official language is not spoken.

9. *Potential students.* An institution may receive sufficient enquiries as to whether or not it offers a particular program such as 'Improve Your Pronunciation' or 'Mandarin for Beginners' to indicate a potential student body for such a program.

10. *Polls.* Polls give an indication of how the public feels towards a social issue and/or towards various aspects of language teaching/learning such as bilingual education, or heritage language maintenance, or the status a language or its speakers has in the community. An awareness of positive and negative attitudes can suggest the need for a public relations program in addition to the language program.

The community as control

Once an area of concern has been recognized it is time to develop a needs analysis to ensure that community resources are spent on a needed and viable program.

Needs analysis

The purpose of a needs analysis is to identify a potential student population and to indicate its linguistic needs. The data may be collected through interviews with counsellors, social workers, teachers, administrators, employers, prospective students and anyone else in the community who has relevant information; or it may be collected through questionnaires or from recent reports.

The kind of descriptive and statistical information that must be assembled is as follows:

- the nature of the target student body, its size, age range, language(s) spoken, socio-economic status, degree of permanent residence with the community or its mobility;
- the purpose for which this group needs language training, such as further education, social interaction, vocational training, career advancement, or travel;
- the specific language skills the students will need in order to achieve this purpose;
- the likely language facility of the students on entry into the program and the desired level on exit;
- the location of the potential student body, its proximity to the institution or to reliable transportation;
- the times when potential students are free to attend class and the need for any special arrangements to release them from other duties;
- the community within which the program will be mounted including the language(s) spoken and their relationship to the target language and, if possible, the probable attitude of the various groups in the community (business, government and private agencies, ethnic groups) towards the potential students and the program;
- the effect the language program might have on the lives of those taking the program and on the community.

This information must be carefully collected. Sloppy work may result in a good program with no students, or in a program which does not fit the students' needs, or in one which is not acceptable to an influential group in the community.

Planning the program

Using the information gathered, the program planners then face the task of establishing the overall objectives of the program, taking into account the views (a) of prospective students; (b) of society as represented by elected officials, community workers, minority group leaders, and others; (c) of policy makers and administrators of the institution that will mount the program; and (d) of the teachers who will work in the program. There must be a reasonable measure of agreement between these groups as to the objectives of the program or dissension will wreck it before it has a chance to prove itself. It is better to spend time talking things over than fighting things through.

The next step is to establish the program goals. As these may be evaluated, they should be stated very explicitly so that internal or external evaluators will, at a later date, be able to state whether or not the goals were attained. The planners should differentiate between 'means goals' or process and 'ends goals' or product. They should also defend the goals from criticism by showing how the students and the community will benefit if the goals are attained.

More detailed planning can then take place that addresses various facets of the program, always bearing in mind the stated objectives and goals:

Design
— format
— scheduling of classes
— size of classes
— content of program
— emphasis within the program
— limits of the program

Administration
— budget
— funding
— fee structure
— recruitment of students
— hiring and supervision of staff
— evaluation of program, formative and summative
— consideration of problems that might arise

Instructional concerns
— criteria for admission
— curriculum planning
— pre-program planning arrangements
— resources (human and material)
— consideration of problems that might arise

79

Evaluation procedures
– criteria for evaluation
– aspects to be evaluated: student progress, instructor performance, curriculum design, cost effectiveness, administrative efficiency, etc.
– design of the evaluation instruments
– recipients of the report

Public relations

New language programs need the support of two communities: 1) members of the institution which is going to mount the program and 2) members of the local community such as parents, community workers, elected representatives, community leaders and taxpayers. The more internal and external support there is for a program, the greater is the possibility of success. The following are some suggestions for obtaining and retaining support:

(a) *Try to get a measure of the attitudes in the institution and in the community towards the proposed program and the students it will serve.*

This may be done formally through a questionnaire or interviews or less formally through conversations and spontaneous feedback. It is helpful to have a sense, right from the beginning, as to how the program may be received.

There are some members of the teaching profession and of the public who have negative attitudes towards second-language-teaching programs. Their reasons are founded in such variables as their mother tongue, their membership in a particular cultural group, their geographical location, their personal experiences with language learning and with speakers of other languages, as well as their perception as to how their tax money should be spent. Changing people's attitudes is not easy. Indeed, some efforts to do so result in the individual becoming even more intransigent. For those whose attitudes are not hardened beyond repair, the following suggestions may produce positive results in some people:

1. Mix together speakers of different languages in social gatherings, public meetings, or classroom exchanges. Once speakers of different languages find that they can communicate, even in a limited way, and that they do have interesting and important things to say to each other, language learning assumes greater importance.

2. Invite the public into a language-teaching classroom. Language teachers are often asked, 'How do you teach a second language?', particularly by older people brought up on the grammar–translation method. Show them and let them take part in a lesson. People understand better what they experience than what is told to them.

3. If you are bilingual, use yourself as a model and demonstrate the advantages of speaking more than one language.
4. Put on a film or lecture series. Good public information sessions employing films, lectures or panel discussions can get across information that may start people revising their attitudes towards language teaching or towards speakers of a particular language.
5. Counter wrong or misleading information whether spoken to you personally or embodied in print. Misinformation which is not challenged immediately is quickly accepted as truth.

(b) *Use institutional and public input as you develop the objectives and design of the program.*

Although this process may seem agonizingly slow at times, it is worth it if consensus is reached, otherwise the program you spend hours developing on your own may be thrown out in a matter of minutes because you did not take the concerns of others into account.

(c) *Develop strategies for explaining the program to the community and for advertising it to prospective students.*

These two aims can often be carried out simultaneously. First, specify the objective of your campaign. Second, identify the various groups in the community you want to reach. Third, decide whether a low-keyed or a high-powered approach would be most appropriate. Fourth, consider the many strategies open to you and pick two or three that you think would work the best.

Possible courses of action are as follows:
– public lectures
– film festival
– language fair or carnival
– ethnic celebration or special day
– modern language week
– book exhibit
– foreign language club
– radio and television commercials
– news releases
– slogans
– bumper stickers
– career clinic
– open house
– forums
– fund-raising activities
– personal encounters

(d) *Recognize the importance of good timing.*

Don't announce your program at a time when it will be overshadowed by a larger and more important program, or immediately after taxpayers have reluctantly agreed to fund a similar program. It may be better to wait six months for a more propitious moment.

(e) *Maintain good relationships with those who can affect the program for good or ill.*

There may be some people within your institution or within the community who have the power to affect your program favorably or adversely. Try to understand their concerns and to work cooperatively towards solutions.

(f) *Develop good communication networks with your colleagues and people in the community.*

Relate your language-teaching curriculum to other subject areas if that is possible. Develop good articulation between your program and other programs in the institution. Parents and community workers and leaders should similarly be kept well-informed if their support is to be won and maintained.

(g) *Try to get some well-known people to endorse your program.*

It helps to have either an expert in the field or a respected politician or citizen endorse your program. We live in an age of advertising and cannot ignore its potential.

(h) *Be ready to justify different aspects of your program.*

Each person who criticizes your program will do it from a different perspective. Have your answers ready to the following questions:
– How will the program benefit the students and the community?
– Why is the program needed?
– What is unique about it?
– Will it be cost-effective?
– Does it have a sound basis in theory?
– Will both the process and the product be evaluated?
– To whom will the program implementors be accountable?

Evaluating the program

When community resources, human and material, are used to mount a program, the institution must expect to be held accountable for the use it has made of those resources, otherwise future support may not be forthcoming. While large programs may be able to build into their budget the cost of a formal evaluation, small programs may have to be content with a less formal evaluation, but one which will, nonetheless, indicate to the institution and the community the degree of success in reaching the program goals.

The following is a standard six-point procedure for evaluating a program:

1. *Issues.* What questions should be asked about the program?
2. *Information.* What information should be collected in order to answer the issue questions and from whom should it be collected?
3. *Method.* How should the information be collected? Who will design any instrument that might be used?
4. *Time.* Over what period of time will the information be collected and analyzed?
5. *Analysis.* How will the data be analyzed? What criteria will be used? What comparisons will be made?
6. *Reporting.* How will the findings be reported? Who will receive the report?

There are different degrees of claims that an evaluation can make for a program beginning with a simple description and ending with a claim for direct responsibility for changes in student behavior:

(a)   This is what we do in this program.
(b)   This is how well we do it.
(c)   This is how well we do it compared to last year.
(d)   This is how much it costs us to do what we do.
(e)   We do what we do better than/cheaper than other people, or if we had chosen another option.
(f)   Our program meets a real community need.
(g)   This is how our program's effectiveness compares with that of another program.
(h)   Not only are there observable changes but our program caused those changes.[10]

Any report which is a public document is also an act of public relations. It may be that the same report sent to a variety of agencies or individuals may not be the best public relations in all cases. While a government department may be interested in a detailed, statistical report, a politician with limited time may prefer a short, succinct summary. A formal, impersonal report may impress some people, while a more intimate case-study approach may be preferred by others. It may seem like a lot of work to prepare two or three differently structured reports, but good community relations have to be worked at in order to gain trust and respect for the educational institution, its programs and its teachers. A report should, as far as possible, answer the questions likely to be raised by an individual or agency in a manner which is intelligible and straightforward. In particular the report should clearly demonstrate the benefits of the program to the students and the community. In the past, teachers have been reluctant to point out the value of the work they do, assuming, perhaps, that no one questions the value of education. But those days are past. Everywhere teachers are under attack, as are other professionals. It behoves teachers to lay out clearly the contribution of their work to society if they hope to retain the present level of funding for educational programs, let alone get increased funding, and to exercise some control over their professional activities.

Activities

1. Compare three different child-rearing practices and comment on their possible effects on language teaching/learning. The comparison might be between child-rearing practices in different countries or in different groups in your community.
2. Examine the aims and objectives of either (a) a professional organization of language teachers, or (b) a language-teacher preservice preparation program. By what means do they seek to attain their objectives and how successful are they?
3. Report on a pressure group active within your community. What are its goals and role? How will its activities affect the community and language-teaching programs?
4. Using the items listed as characteristics of students, teachers, curriculum and program in Section 3.3, draw up a 'Profile of control' for your language-teaching situation showing those areas where you exercise no control, some control, or total control.
5. Plan and, if possible, run a workshop according to the suggestions made on an area of language teaching in which you have particular expertise.
6. Research an issue in the community which has some connection with language teaching: the institution or district budget; maintenance of heritage languages; population decline or increase; attitudes towards other languages and cultures; or political party platforms or policies.
7. Draw up a needs assessment for a language program that is desirable in your community. If possible, conduct the assessment.
8. Outline a public relations program for getting and maintaining community support for an ongoing or proposed language program.

4 National policies and language teaching

This chapter will examine the effects of various national policies on second language teaching and suggest ways in which language teachers can work with communities in making changes to educational practices and policies.

4.1 Overview

National policies are established in a number of ways: by official government decree, by customs or tradition, by a vocal and powerful group, by paternalism, or by prejudice. Policies arise out of the geography and history of a country. A country located where trading routes converge will have a different history from one isolated from the effects of modern civilization. A country repeatedly ravaged by war will have developed differently from one which has been fortunate enough to remain neutral. A country peopled by one race professing one religion will not have experienced the tensions of a nation containing different races, religions, languages and cultures. A detailed study of the history and geography of the country in which they are teaching, whether it is their own country or another, will provide language teachers with many insights into why things are the way they are in second language education, and foster a greater tolerance for what is. It may also help language teachers to plan realistically for the future, knowing that both the past and the present affect what is to come.

After the Second World War education expanded rapidly all over the world. In recent years that growth has slowed down, perhaps because of economic recession, perhaps because of uncertainty regarding the nature and role of education in various societies. During the years of expansion education underwent changes not only in quantity and quality but also in philosophy and methodology. Second language teaching grew from a corner store operation to big business with a wide range of programs and methodologies. Because second language learning/teaching affects the lives of individuals, communities, and nations it has been and will continue to be susceptible to changes in national policies.

This chapter will begin (4.2) by considering the effects of national policies in the following four areas of language teaching: emigration/ immigration, education, language rights, and the economy and employment. The next section (4.3) will look at ways in which teachers can become politically informed, while the last section (4.4) will examine methods by which teachers can work with various individuals and groups in making necessary changes to educational practices and policies.

4.2 The effects of national policies

Emigration/immigration policies

The migration of people from one part of their land to another (internal migration) or from one part of the world to another (international migration) is a recurring event throughout history. From the movement of pre-historic man over the face of the earth until today, the human condition seems to demand mobility as both a right and an opportunity to improve on that condition.

Migration can be planned or unplanned, voluntary or involuntary, internal or international. The building of the Aswan Dam required the planned removal of those who lived in the area to be flooded; the flight of the Hungarians from their homes was unplanned. Independent immigrants decide on their own volition to leave their countries; refugees have no choice. The rural poor hope to find economic security within the growing industrial cities in their homelands; others seek financial security beyond their national boundaries.

During the latter part of the last century and the early decades of this century, thousands of people, largely unskilled or semi-skilled, migrated from Europe to North and South America and Australia to break new land and to work in the factories. Governments welcomed both their leaving and their coming, and placed few controls on these huge movements of people across the oceans. Immigration from Asia was either banned or given a low quota at this time and did not open up until after the close of the Second World War.

During this post-war period, governments have exercised much greater control over both emigration and immigration. Eastern European governments do not readily permit their nationals to leave their homelands, while Western European governments place few, if any, restrictions on who may emigrate. Language teachers in receiving countries may therefore meet many students from some countries and few students from others.

There are factors which push people out of their own country – political unrest, economic instability, famine, war, unemployment; and factors which pull them towards another country – security, freedom, employment, social and educational mobility. The four common reasons why people wish to leave their country either permanently or for an extended stay abroad are as follows:

1. to better themselves and their families economically;
2. to be reunited with their families already established overseas;
3. to study at a foreign institution;
4. to seek refuge from political, economic or religious strife or persecution.

A major cause of both internal and external migration is economic insecurity. There are two ways of looking at poverty levels. One is to ask: how little does an individual need to subsist on? The other is to ask: how much does an individual need in order that his/her standard of living compares favorably with that of others? Proponents of the first way, subsistence poverty, fix the poverty level at the minimum people need for basic housing, clothing and food. Proponents of the second way, relative poverty, fix the poverty level higher to take into account the special needs of families and their natural desire to enjoy a lifestyle considered normal in their community. In some parts of the world hundreds of thousands of people live below the subsistence poverty level, suffering severe malnutrition with little hope of a better future. But the push of poverty and the pull of the prospect, no matter how faint, of a better standard of living in the burgeoning industrial cities keeps alive the steady flow of people from rural to urban areas within the same nation. These internal migrants may well experience many of the attributes of culture shock usually associated with international migration as they face a new culture embedded in urban living and, in multilingual countries, possibly a new language. For those living above the subsistence level, the goal is often to reach the standard of living enjoyed by those in the developed countries of Europe, North America and Australia where the possession of large material items such as cars, television sets and, increasingly, computers is taken for granted as being part of 'the good life'. For some of them, international voluntary migration offers a way to increased economic security.

The unequal distribution of wealth throughout the world is matched by the unequal distribution of the population between the developed and less developed countries. The less developed countries account for about 70 percent of the world's population today, and of the possible additional two billion that may be added by the end of the century, about 90 percent will live in the less developed countries. The current and anticipated population explosion places pressures on governments to try to limit the population growth and on agriculture and industry to try to supply people's needs. Medical science has increased the life span of people all over the world and decreased the child mortality rate. In developing countries a high percentage of the population, perhaps 40 percent in some cases, is under eighteen and approaching the child-bearing years signalling the prospect of a further increase in population. Meanwhile in the developed countries where population growth is close to zero, more people are living longer and must be housed, fed and cared for through services that will be paid for by taxes from the lesser number of productive citizens. So while the developing nations may have a surfeit of labor for the coming decades, the developed nations may be short, and the migration of workers from one part of the world to another may continue to be a fact of life.

Death rates have dropped because of the imposition upon people by their governments and private agencies of improved sanitation and preventive medicine. Birth control cannot be so easily imposed as it necessitates individuals making personal decisions to limit the size of their families which may require that values, traditions and patterns of behavior which have been passed on for generations must be replaced. The People's Republic of China has initiated a population control program by a system of rewards and penalties which encourage parents to have no more than one child. Developed countries cannot, however, ignore the pressures that build up in areas where the population growth exceeds the ability of the authorities to deal with it effectively. Migration from overpopulated underdeveloped areas to underpopulated developed areas will not be sufficient to eliminate that mounting tension, but unless the developed nations make some effort to relieve unnecessary suffering and frustration they will ultimately suffer the consequences.

Many nations have operated highly discriminatory immigration policies often through a quota system. The justification was usually one of self-interest: 1) the country was not prepared to accept large numbers of people from another part of the world such that the dominance of the host society by one race or religion would be challenged; or 2) the country would not accept sick, handicapped or unskilled people who might be a drain on the public purse; or 3) the country would not accept in any one year more immigrants than it felt the economy and the society could absorb. While the major receiving countries have more liberal policies than they did two or three decades ago, they do not permit open, unrestricted immigration and have enacted various laws to deal with illegal immigration. Immigration is now regulated by most receiving countries to conform with national economic development policies and, to some degree, humanistic principles.

Immigration has always been tied to manpower. When unskilled labor was needed, laborers were welcome. Today selection procedures in most receiving nations stress skills or investment capital as these lie at the base of increased national productivity. Countries short of manpower encourage two kinds of immigrants: those whom they are prepared at some time in the future to accept as citizens, and seasonal workers who will be expected to return home once the demand for their labor is satisfied. Those who immigrate permanently usually bring their families or the family comes later as most receiving countries have a policy which permits the reunification of families.

Immigration that is tied to a receiving nation's economy rises and falls in tune with its booms and recessions, making the planning of second language programs for immigrants difficult on a long-term basis. Some countries attempt to fix the total number of immigrants that will be accepted in one year, but they cannot guarantee that the number will be met nor can they guarantee where the immigrants will ultimately settle. As a result, ESL programs for adults are often seen as a temporary phenomenon which creates a sense of insecurity in ESL teachers. Similarly planning ahead for ESL programs in schools for the children of immigrants is difficult when the number who may be seeking admission in the following year can only be roughly estimated. While it may be possible to extrapolate from projected immigration figures the approximate percentage that will be at or near school age, many children born in the receiving country of immigrant parents may grow up in homes where the official language is not spoken and this number is hard to calculate.

There has been a considerable change in the major source countries of voluntary immigrants. One reason is pragmatic: if it is to their economic advantage, receiving nations will take skilled workers or professionals or those with investment capital from any country that is prepared to let them go. The second reason is more humanistic: the blatant racist policies of the first four decades of this century are no longer acceptable in a world where mass suffering is depicted daily on millions of television screens and where human rights movements have focused attention on discrimination and deprivation. New selection policies have opened the doors to immigrants from Asia and Africa and third-world countries on an unprecedented scale, resulting in new challenges for host communities, and new challenges for second language teachers who now work with people from a variety of linguistic and cultural backgrounds. These policies must also bear some responsibility for the 'brain drain' from countries which can ill afford to let their educated elite go. It is, however, understandable that highly educated professional people prefer to carry on their work in countries where equipment, trained personnel and funds are available, and where political and economic conditions are fairly stable.

The more humanistic approach to immigration can also be seen in the increase in both quantity and quality of services to immigrants in language training and settlement. Language classes and counselling and information services are usually available free or at a low cost in the major receiving countries, and, while the reasons for providing them may be political rather than altruistic these services contribute much to the quick and easy adjustment of immigrants to their new homeland. Many countries encourage immigrants to take out citizenship papers after living in the host country for a certain number of years and perhaps passing a citizenship test.

During this century alone, migration due to strife has forced the relocation of millions of people around the world. Civil war or international war have both produced their permanently displaced persons. Political and religious discrimination and oppression have seen an exodus of people from their homelands to countries where freedom is cherished. In the post-war years we have watched the migration of people from East Germany, Hungary, Czechoslovakia, Poland, Russia, Uganda, Chile, Argentina, Cuba and Vietnam to mention only the better-known cases. Without doubt we shall see more migrations before the century is out.

Political and economic strife lie behind the great refugee movements of the past forty years. By 1949 the refugee problem was so acute that the United Nations Organization established the Office of the United Nations High Commissioner for Refugees (UNHCR). This office lies at the center of a network of government and private agencies, both national and international, which assist refugees. In addition, the UNHCR publicizes both the problems faced by refugees and the activities undertaken on their behalf. It obtains its funds from national governments and private agencies or foundations and may spend many millions of dollars in one year providing the necessary relief. Some of the agencies the UNHCR works with are the Intergovernmental Committee for Migration (ICM), the International Committee of the Red Cross (ICRC), the International Council of Voluntary Agencies (ICVA), and various church and national councils or agencies.

Involuntary, unplanned migrations of refugees, the kind that result from poverty, famine or strife, may erupt quickly and affect first those countries bordering the source of the trouble. Without help from the UNHCR and private agencies, the receiving country, which may itself be facing economic hardship, is placed under a tremendous burden to supply the immediate physical necessities of life to non-citizens. Quickly the refugee camps can become permanent and perhaps dehumanizing centers where children grow up knowing nothing except insecurity and hopelessness. Getting refugees out of these camps occurs when the refugees agree to voluntary repatriation, or the first receiving country agrees to allow the refugees to settle there and become integrated, or another country agrees to accept the refugees as immigrants and to assist in their resettlement.

But nations are by no means prepared to accept anyone who is designated a refugee. Admission qualifications vary from country to country. Refugees who have a marketable skill or who speak the language of the receiving country are usually given preference. Those who have family overseas may be given priority if the country follows a policy of reunification of families.

For some refugees, training in the language of their new country may begin in the refugee camp while they are waiting for their papers to be processed, but many must wait until they reach their destination. Once they arrive in the host country, refugees may undergo orientation lasting a few days or a few weeks at a center established for that purpose. Here health problems are checked and relocation plans finalized. Language programs may be offered if the stay is long enough, but eventually the refugees will arrive in the community that is to be their home. A host family or a committee for refugee settlement may be on hand to greet the newcomers and to help them through the period of adjustment that must ensue. Ethnic organizations may also help by providing assistance in the refugees' own language.

Usually language training begins soon after arrival both for the children and adults and may be subsidized by the government. For public/state schools, an influx of refugee children may create problems in both staffing and space. In addition, the children may come from a culture not previously encountered by the school. The Vietnamese children were a case in point: teachers and counsellors had much to learn about the Vietnamese culture and were often unaware of the difference between true Vietnamese people and the ethnic Chinese who lived in Vietnam and were also refugees. Many of these children had gone through some terrible experiences seeing their parents, brothers and sisters killed in the fighting or lost at sea and were in a state of shock which only time, security and acceptance could cure. Language teachers had to be patient as the trauma slowly died away and the children could look forward to a better future. After receiving successive waves of refugee children during the last four decades, school districts in large cities can usually mount language programs fairly quickly calling on experienced trained teachers. In rural areas the lack of expertise is, to some degree, compensated for by a strong community spirit of support for the incoming family.

Language training for adults begins with 'survival' language to enable the refugees to find their way about the community and to conduct simple transactions. Later, language training may form a component of educational upgrading or vocational training. Refugee women often have difficulty obtaining second language instruction for two reasons: 1) they may not be destined for the workforce and therefore do not qualify under skill-giving government programs; and 2) they may come from a culture which expects women to stay at home.

Although the first year of life in a new country is undoubtedly one of stress, community support, both material and human, is usually forthcoming. But as the excitement of newness dies down and support dwindles, refugees can experience a period of defeat and depression as they struggle to build a place for themselves. Some succeed and become established; some fail and may need extensive counselling.

While language teachers working with refugees will be engaged in classroom teaching and curriculum building, they can expect to play three other roles: friend, informant, and counsellor. The language teacher is often the first person within the new community with whom the refugee has a close relationship. The warmth of the initial reception, the trust that is engendered, and the empathy that is apparent all help the refugee to overcome some of the trauma of the preceding months which may include

– the preflight experience involving the perception of a threat to life or liberty, the decision to flee, and the dangers and emotions of the flight;
– the initial relief on reaching safety followed by the boredom and frustration of camp life;
– the eventual resettlement with its necessary adjustments to a new culture and language.

For some the harsh experiences are never fully overcome and bring on emotional and physical health problems. No language teacher can ignore the sequence of events which has led to the resettlement of migrants, for these are part and parcel of the individual and will affect his/her classroom performance.

Changing emigration–immigration policies and refugee movements have affected language teachers as professionals and as private citizens:

1. Because immigration figures fluctuate according to world and national political and economic situations, some second-language-teaching jobs tend to lack long-term security.

2. Because source countries have changed, some language teachers now teach students from a wider variety of linguistic and cultural backgrounds.

3. Because governments are showing more open concern for the settlement of immigrants, the job of teaching immigrants has risen in prestige.

4. Because of greater concern for immigrants and increased funding for programs, second language teachers have been able to mount a wider variety of programs, for example, programs for speakers of specific languages, or for workers in specific trades or professions, or for those applying for citizenship.

5. Because they have been exposed to the tragic stories of refugees, language teachers' views of the world and of their personal responsibilities to others have been affected.

Education policies

Three terms are frequently used in education: aims, goals, policies. Aims are value-laden. They arise out of a particular philosophy or a belief in a particular value system. They direct attention to what is considered desirable. Goals concern the end product of education – what it is hoped will be attained as a result of the process of education. Policies regulate the internal operation of the educational system and the relationship of the system to other systems. Policies provide a sense of day-to-day continuity. Because policies have a prescriptive force and must cope with the different interests of a heterogeneous society, they arouse controversy. Policies can make a significant difference to people's lives. Unfortunately, because policies affect people, not inanimate objects, the consequences of new policies – the intensity and breadth of their effects – cannot always be judged accurately prior to their implementation. However, policies are – or should be – open to re-evaluation and subsequent change.

The legitimacy of the educational system is rooted in political authority which regulates its actions through policies and provides its resources. Ministers of education are politicians, not pedagogues. Indeed, they may know very little about the process of education; their task is to make political rather than pedagogical decisions. A minister's authority is given by the legislature which sets the policies that he/she must implement. The minister then gives directives to administrators who, in turn, put these into practice in the schools and colleges. Administrators who want to implement a particular program must, therefore, at some time convince politicians that the program will be instrumental in meeting the goals of a particular aim, because what ultimately structures education is not the wish of an administrator but the will of the public expressed through their elected representatives. When the public is not satisfied with the educational system, it can show its displeasure by not re-electing the politicians, and by forcing a change of minister.

Educational policies deal with matters of great importance to various segments of the population, but establishing sound educational policies is not easy. First, there is a general inertia that has to be overcome – people just don't want to change. Second, there is often ignorance over viable alternatives to current policies. Third, as it is not always possible to judge the consequences of a change of policy, the uncertainty produced can be inhibiting. Fourth, the realms of politics and its handmaiden, economics, are both unstable, and the calmness needed for the careful consideration of alternative policies may simply not be present. Fifth, the full needs of a community may not be known, but only those of a vociferous minority. Sixth, when a number of different people or different groups all have perfectly legitimate policy proposals in their own spheres of interest, taken together these proposals may be in conflict even though each may sincerely have the best interests of the students at heart.

Educational policies are affected by economic and social policies, as these regulate the amount of money and resources that will be available to institutions as well as establishing the atmosphere that surrounds and permeates them. Sometimes economic and social policies combine to change the direction of education. In North America in the late 1960s and early 1970s the push for social justice and equality of opportunity in education came at a time when the booming economy permitted increased money to be spent on educationally disadvantaged people. New programs, new materials and new buildings were authorized under new policies. That decade also produced policies endorsing multicul- turalism or cultural pluralism and where these were adopted the teaching of languages, both first and second, official and non-official, received increased support. In the sphere of international politics, realignment of some countries caused some major retraining programs for language teachers as the authorized second language was changed to meet the new alliances. The desire on the part of some developing countries for increased industrialization caused them to send thousands of their young people overseas to study. As a result, receiving nations adopted different policies regarding acceptance or non-acceptance of visa students into publicly-funded colleges and universities. Not all these policies were made public: unofficial quota systems can be set by the simple expedient of slowing down the processing of student visa applications, or institu- tions can charge considerably higher fees for out-of-country students, thereby limiting access.

National educational policies affect who teaches what language to whom. The decisions a nation makes can only be understood by examining its history, its socio-economic and cultural characteristics, the status of the languages and cultures of minority groups, and the prevailing attitudes of the public to public issues. Ignorance of the larger arena in which educational policies are made results in ill-formed proposals and uninformed criticism.

An area of education which affects all teachers is that of publishing. Language teachers depend on local, national and international publishing companies for the commercial materials they use in their classes, yet policies regarding which materials will be published, what method they will advocate and what the content will be are rarely formalized. The last two decades have produced a wide range of print and non-print materials for use in language-teaching classrooms. Often the display of materials at a language-teaching convention is overwhelming. Unless teachers have some guidelines by which they can judge the quality and efficacy of the materials, their choice may resemble a lottery. Misleading advertising, exaggerated claims, or a failure to specify the goals and the design of the program and the audience for which it is intended can result in teachers purchasing unsuitable materials. Any free market regulates and governs itself to some degree, but it is consumers who have the power to establish unofficial policies which work to their benefit. For example, since EPIE (Educational Products Information Exchange[1]) was established a few years ago in the United States, more and more publishers and authors are using its criteria when describing their materials knowing that selection committees can request an EPIE analysis before deciding which texts to purchase. EPIE is a carefully worked out system for analyzing and evaluating both print and non-print materials. The analyst tries to answer some very basic questions through a detailed examination of the material: What are the stated goals of the program? Is it likely that the program will achieve those goals? How well do the various parts of the program fit together? Does the program contain bias or prejudice? What are the underlying assumptions? How well will it meet the needs of the teacher and students? When consumers follow a policy of not purchasing materials that do not meet particular criteria, the marketplace adjusts.

The problem of selecting the right materials was not as difficult thirty years ago. In the 1950s when the audio-lingual approach was dominant, one set of texts was very like another. But once the cognitive-code approach broke the hold of the audio-lingual many other approaches were born: the 'silent way', total physical response, CL/CLL (counselling-learning/community language learning), 'suggestopedia', and the communicative approach, to mention a few. The publishing business soon showed a willingness to produce materials based on these new ideas. The underlying assumptions and principles of a set of materials, that is, the method used, can affect the approach, design and procedures used by a teacher in the classroom. However, teachers who had little or no training in the new methods often felt uncomfortable with them and returned to the safety of the audio-lingual texts. Better preservice and inservice teacher training enables teachers to be more discerning in choosing materials which fit with their philosophy of language teaching/learning, and gives them a measure of control over publishing policies as these must be sensitive to the demand.

The growing interest in multiculturalism, cultural pluralism and, in some parts of the world, nationalism has resulted in texts which either cater to one distinct ethnic or national group or, conversely, try to encompass all groups. Pictures reflect faces from around the world as do the names of the characters. Texts are carefully checked for bias or prejudice. Countries which previously used British or American series are now producing their own. Small minority groups within countries, such as the indigenous people, are also writing their own materials for use in heritage language classes. Some countries are exporting materials to teach the ancestral language to the children of their emigrants.

While student texts provide the largest market for publishers, books dealing with the theories behind language teaching in the areas of methodology, linguistics, psycholinguistics, and sociolinguistics have also proliferated as one theory or approach has superseded another. For the untrained teacher the result has been confusion. Who can one believe? The author one has just read or the author one is about to read? Language teaching is no longer the simple straightforward profession it once was when all the beginning instructor appeared to need was a teacher-proof text based on the audio-lingual approach. Nowadays, theory and practice must go hand-in-hand. National policies regarding the training of language teachers affects what is published, for good training programs demand well-written up-to-date texts which combine theory and practice. Thirty years ago there was a handful of such texts; today the choice is large and represents a variety of philosophical, linguistic and pedagogical viewpoints.

All practicing teachers should subscribe to one or more journals dealing with their specific area of interest. Many associations of language teachers, local, national and international, publish newsletters and professional journals. Articles range from the purely theoretical to the practical. This enables teachers to keep easily up-to-date with the latest ideas and controversies within the profession. Funding of these journals often presents a problem, as production costs are high when sales are small. Grants from government and private agencies and subscriptions help to keep journals alive. (For a list of journals and newsletters related to second language teaching see Appendix A.)

CALL (Computer-Assisted Language Learning) is still fairly new in many parts of the world, but indications are that it will become more widespread as the cost of computers decreases and their availability increases. Commercial enterprises are already producing computer materials for use in language classrooms, and while these, as yet, lack the sophistication that more experimentation will undoubtedly bring, they are beginning to have an impact. Politicians and administrators are increasingly recognizing the importance of computers in education. People entering the language-teaching profession will soon have to know computer language in addition to the target language.

National education policies

1. determine what languages shall be taught to whom and by whom and therefore affect (a) the lives of those who do or do not have access to language programs, and (b) the status, hiring, and working conditions of language teachers;

2. give priority to certain educational issues over others and hence determine which programs are supported and which are not;
3. affect the quality of language-teaching programs, including the print and non-print materials available to teachers.

Language rights policies

> The conception of human dignity is fundamentally linked to the life of the mind which in turn is closely linked to language as a basic means of communication. Language is a rudiment of consciousness and close to the core of personality; deprivations in relation to language deeply affect personality....
>
> Deprivations imposed in relation to language may be manifested in a variety of modes, notably: denial of opportunity to acquire and employ the mother tongue, the language of the national elite, or world languages; deprivations imposed upon individuals through group identifications and differentiations effected by language; deprivations resulting from arbitrary requirements of specified languages for access to different value processes (as for employment); the conduct of community processes and enterprises, especially of enlightenment and power, in languages alien to members of the community; and, finally, the coerced learning of specified languages other than the home language.[2]

Throughout history, at various places and at various times, children and adults have been discriminated against because they either speak or do not speak a particular language. In recent decades language rights have come under increasing protection. The Charter of the United Nations lists language along with race, sex, and religion as an impermissible ground for differentiation. In 1948 the United Nations Organization's Universal Declaration of Human Rights again gave language as an impermissible ground for differentiation. It did not, however, explicitly require nations to provide access to a particular language or languages when lack of access would impinge upon other rights such as due process of law, freedom of religion, or the right to an education, to express oneself freely, and to participate in the cultural life of the community. In 1960 the Convention against Discrimination in Education prohibited 'any distinction, exclusion, limitation or preference' on language or any other ground which would result in some children receiving a lower quality of education than other children. This prohibition did not exclude minority groups from setting up their own schools provided that 'this right is not exercised in a manner which prevents the members of these minorities from understanding the culture and language of the community as a whole and from participating in its activities or which prejudices national sovereignty'. This right of minority groups to maintain their languages was further recognized in 1966 by article 27 of the Covenant on Civil and Political Rights adopted by the United Nations Organization.[3]

It was not too long before language rights were tested in the law courts of Europe and North America. One of the most famous was the Lau vs. Nichols case in the United States. A class action was filed by thirteen non-English-speaking students, seven of whom were born in the United States, on behalf of nearly 3,000 Chinese-speaking students in the San Francisco Unified School District. The claim was made that these non-English-speaking students were being denied the right to an education because they could not function in the language of the school, English, and that, as a result, they were doomed to become dropouts and to suffer prolonged unemployment because of their failure to acquire an adequate education. The case finished up in the US Supreme Court where, on January 21, 1974, the court ruled that the failure of the school district to provide English language instruction to non-English-speaking children denied them the opportunity to participate in the educational program and hence violated their right to equal educational opportunity as guaranteed by the Constitution of the United States and by the State of California. The court said:

> There is no equality of treatment merely by providing students with the same facilities, textbooks, teachers, and curriculum; for students who do not understand English are effectively foreclosed from any meaningful education.
>
> Basic English skills are at the very core of what these public schools teach. Imposition of a requirement that before a child can effectively participate in the education program he must have already acquired these basic skills is to make a mockery of public education.[4]

While the decision of the court did not specifically call for bilingual education, many districts interpreted it that way. Consequently, the number of bilingual education programs has increased rapidly since that historic finding.

The Lau vs. Nichols case seemed to establish three principles:

1. that school districts in the United States do have a legal responsibility for providing programs appropriate to the special needs of non-English-speaking students;

2. that providing all students, regardless of their special needs, with exactly the same service is not equivalent to providing equality of opportunity;

3. that students should receive equal benefits from the educational process which is, of course, denied them if they do not understand the language of instruction.

While increased language rights in education for the children of minority groups makes a lot of sense pedagogically, there are many people who feel that once immigrants make the decision to leave their homeland and settle in a new country, they should give up their first language and refrain from passing it on to their children. Heinz Kloss offers four theories which may lie behind people's reasoning, and then refutes each theory, as summarised below:

1. *The tacit compact theory*

This theory claims that at the time the immigrants apply for admission to the host country and the host country admits them, the two parties conclude a compact tacitly implying that in exchange for entering the host country the immigrants are prepared to adapt to the new culture and language and waive their claim to any minority rights.

But Kloss points out that the theory is not in keeping with the facts. The major receiving nations in North and South America, Britain and Australia have always permitted immigrants to establish heritage language schools.

2. *The take and give theory*

This theory claims that most immigrants will become more prosperous economically than they were in their homeland, and that in return they should give themselves wholeheartedly to their adopted country, including giving up their language and culture.

This theory fails to recognize the contribution that immigrants make to the economy. While many first generation immigrants may only be able to contribute unskilled labor, this helps to expand the consumer market. Kloss directs attention to the many immigrants who have added new dimensions to the economy by setting up new industries and by using their professional skills. Immigrants should not be expected to give up their cultural and linguistic heritage in addition to giving their skills and their labor to the host country.

3. *The anti-ghettoization theory*

According to this theory, the passing on of a minority language from one generation to another locks each generation up in a sterile cultural ghetto secluded from the mainstream of national life.

While this can be a danger, Kloss does not feel it need necessarily be so. Wise language policies will ensure that minority groups have access to the majority language and culture while maintaining their own heritage. It is not an either/or situation.

4. *The national unity theory*

This theory claims that because immigrant groups which perpetuate their language may become a politically disruptive force, the host country has the right to require linguistic assimilation.

Kloss admits there is some truth to the notion that linguistically heterogeneous nations are less stable than linguistically homogeneous nations, but the cause may lie not in the linguistic heterogeneity but in discriminatory treatment accorded the minorities by the majority group. Injustice produces unrest which provides governments with reasons for restrictive policies.[5]

Many nations are still formulating language rights policies and having these tested in the courts. Some policies promote the use of particular languages in the public domain for activities connected with such concerns as government, law and education. Other policies simply tolerate the use by minorities of their own language in those domains not under the control of public authorities such as ethnic newspapers, heritage language schools, and religious services.

National language rights policies increase or decrease opportunities for speakers of non-official languages

1. to obtain an education equivalent to, though not necessarily the same as, that received by speakers of the official language(s) by receiving services appropriate to their needs;
2. to maintain their first language and culture;
3. to have equal access with speakers of the official language(s) to the power structure, to employment, and to various processes and activities of the wider community.

The issue of language rights has implications for language teachers. When language rights as recommended by the United Nations Organization are upheld, jobs open up in language teaching, in curriculum development, and in research.

Economic and employment policies

There seems to be a two-way relationship between educational expansion on the one hand, and economic growth, and therefore increased employment opportunities on the other hand. John W. Meyer and Michael T. Hannon point to various writers who claim that 'in more industrialized countries labor markets are more thoroughly organized around educational credentials, education becomes more of a human capital investment, and the traditional criteria of status and prestige become less important than in non-industrialized countries. Consequently, individuals desire and demand more schooling to increase their own economic reward.'[6] Other writers counter this by claiming that 'Evidence from non-industrialized countries, however, suggests that labor markets there are also highly organized by educational credentials, that individual rates of return on education are not necessarily lower, and that traditional criteria of status and prestige may not be more valued than in industrialized countries.'[7] The authors further point out that 'Development strategies vary across countries, but every national elite understands that the development process requires rational planning and technically trained personnel.'[8]

Improved language skills may be the key to jobs for the unemployed or to better jobs for the underemployed. As vocational skills can be learned along with language skills, it is possible to design programs with both objectives in mind. For these programs to be effective, there must be long-term planning that will determine what kind and what numbers of skilled or semi-skilled workers will be needed in the near or more distant future, and what language skills foreign workers should have in order to be safe and productive members of the workforce. These decisions will be based on the kind and amount of job creation envisaged by industry and government, taking into account national and world economic forecasts.

Vocational training programs that have a built-in language component may take place on a job site when a particular employer co-operates with an educational institution in mounting a program that will either 1) assist present employees in changing their jobs or seeking promotion or 2) train prospective employees; or courses may be held off-site at a vocational training institution. Training programs that do not have a built-in language component may, through their entrance requirements, discriminate against adults who do not have facility in the language of instruction even though they may have the requisite technical knowledge and skills.

Vocational training programs for people of limited language ability can seldom be cost-recoverable as the clients are, for the most part, in the low-income bracket. Indeed, they can be costly to run as they involve client recruitment and selection, program planning, the purchase of materials, assessment, counselling and placement of trainees and sometimes the payment of a subsistence allowance. Only a national policy to underwrite such programs can ensure that they will be mounted.

Both overt and covert discrimination continue to be practiced in some countries in the employment field. More women are found in lower-paid jobs than men. Certain jobs are more likely to be filled by members of one ethnic group than another. Top management jobs go to people 'just like us'. Credentials obtained in one country are not accepted in another country even though they may be just as good or better. 'Local experience' is cited as a necessary criterion to obtain a position when, in fact, all that is needed is a short orientation to the job. Policies which require public and private agencies to hire members of minority groups, be they women or blacks or the unemployed, attempt to redress previous discrimination by what seems to some to be reverse discrimination, that is, jobs are reserved for members of minority groups at the expense of members of the majority group. Results are twofold: 1) new jobs are created for members of minority groups providing them with an opportunity to prove themselves but 2) resentment builds within the majority group which sees its members being denied jobs for which they feel as well, if not better, qualified. The measure of a civilization, however, should not be in its wealth but in the care it provides for its disadvantaged citizens, for the physically and mentally handicapped, for the poor, and for the unemployed, regardless of what language they speak.

Immigrants who are seeking to better themselves must make decisions regarding their future which require that they have access to information relevant to those decisions. Information centers have been one means by which newcomers can find out how to apply for a job or what their rights are as members of the workforce or of trade unions. However, migrants often need to be oriented towards a society which may differ considerably in some fundamental ways from their own. They need careful counselling so that they fully understand the options open to them and the consequences for employment or promotion which may follow a particular decision. Good orientation and counselling services can help people to find satisfactory employment.

There is no doubt that a healthy economy benefits language teachers. When the national coffers are full there is money for education, but, as the coffers empty, programs seen as non-essential – and language programs are often included in this category – are cut. A healthy economy also results in people having money in their pockets to spend on travel, which sometimes motivates them to learn another language if only at the survival level. A healthy economy means increased international trade. Business people need to be prepared to transact deals in other languages and other cultures. Native speakers of major languages are employed to teach their language and the subtleties of the paralanguage to business people preparing to go abroad. But when a nation's economy sags, not only does business drop off, but immigration decreases causing some second language teachers to lose their jobs as classes are closed. However, enlightened national policies regarding second language training and vocational training for unemployed or underemployed adults result in the establishment of funded programs employing both language teachers and vocational instructors.

4.3 Becoming informed politically

Becoming informed politically does not necessarily involve joining a political party; it does involve understanding public affairs which impinge upon second language teaching and perhaps taking sides. As

has been shown, language classrooms do not operate in isolation from the various communities which surround them. It therefore behoves language teachers to develop a political awareness and sensitivity if they want to play a part in making decisions that will benefit their students. Language teachers need to be informed on at least some of the following points:
- the philosophies underlying the actions of relevant educational institutions, public and private agencies, political parties, and pressure groups;
- the policies proclaimed and practiced by these groups;
- the power bases within the community;
- the unmet needs of individuals and organizations within the community;
- emerging trends within the community;
- means and lines of communication within the community;
- the history of the issue currently under discussion;
- strategies which have proved effective or ineffective in the past.

There are four major sources of information on the political climate surrounding a language-teaching issue: the media, reports, committee and public meetings, and networks.

THE MEDIA

Newspapers, magazines, journals, radio and television bombard us with information such that information storage and retrieval is very big business. John Naisbitt wrote, 'The new source of power is not money in the hands of a few but information in the hands of many.'[9] For language teachers, becoming informed on matters which do not appear at first glance to be central to classroom teaching may take a back seat unless they plan carefully what they will read and view so as to ensure a reasonable coverage of important, relevant issues. Teachers should endeavour to subscribe to a local and national newspaper and/or magazine, listen regularly to newscasts, and view documentary films. As media reports usually reflect the bias of either the reporter or the reporter's employer, it is very important that any issue be looked at from different points of view.

REPORTS

Reports act as concrete reference points which can be pointed to when the need arises. The major sources of reports are:
1. government ministries or departments such as those that deal with education or immigration or employment;
2. educational institutions from kindergarten through university;

3. private agencies such as those that provide information and counselling services to members of minority groups whether indigenous or immigrant;
4. task forces set up by official bodies to study a specific topic such as the teaching of languages to children;
5. independent pressure groups such as those seeking to have a modern language taught in primary school.

Reports serve different functions:

1. *Statistical information.* Governments in particular issue reports giving for instance, the number of people emigrating from or immigrating to a country, or the number employed or unemployed. These statistics may suggest trends which will later affect language teachers.
2. *Policy papers.* Governments and institutions like to test public opinion by issuing papers outlining proposed new policy. Reaction which follows may well modify the proposed policy thereby producing a law which is more acceptable to those it will affect. Silence is usually taken to mean assent.
3. *Policy statements.* Once a policy has been passed by the governing body, a statement may be issued clarifying the policy for those who are affected by it.
4. *Research reports.* Research carried on in trade and industry, in social services, and in other facets of the public domain may assist language teachers in program planning. For example, polls on the attitude of the public to bilingual education enable educators to see the strength of the opposition they face. Research into technology, particularly the use and cost of computers, may affect curriculum design.

COMMUNITY COMMITTEES AND PUBLIC MEETINGS

It is often said that the best way to deal with dissenters is to put them on committees so that 1) they may fully understand the complexity and ramifications of the problem for which they were offering simplistic solutions; or 2) they may become acquainted with opposing views which have merit; or 3) they may take issue with the stalling techniques and/or general incompetency of the committee and produce change. Service on a community committee can be an informing and rewarding experience resulting in new programs for the community and new friends and colleagues for the committee members.

Public meetings can also be highly informative as the various speakers, both those on the platform and those in the audience, address the issue from various viewpoints. Public meetings provide language teachers with a forum in which they can present the views of professional educators.

NETWORKS

Networking is an old phenomenon which, as result of the breakdown of some of the established hierarchical administrative structures coupled with the information explosion, has recently gained strength. It is an attempt to solve the problem of how people can exchange information and share ideas with those they trust.

The old hierarchical system was a vertical system which encouraged people to move up and get ahead with perhaps little thought for those who must necessarily be pushed down. The system produced stress and anxiety and did not allow for free exchange of information, for information is power. Networks, on the other hand, move horizontally. Colleagues in the network system trust each other and look to each other for support rather than to a supervisor. Networks link individuals to individuals, individuals to organizations, and organizations to organizations. The process involves the decentralization of information by providing horizontal access to it.

Two individuals or two organizations can set up a network which they can expand quickly or slowly according to their resources. Networks should guard against becoming too large too quickly: first, because funding the newsletter (or whatever means of information dissemination is used) can become a problem and, second because members of a large organization often feel out of touch, something networking was supposed to cure not cause.

A network should be initiated for a particular purpose, that is, there should be one common denominator which binds all the members together. It may be
– a personal characteristic such as age or sex
– a vocation or profession
– a topic
– a cause
Networks are not self-sustaining. They have to be well organized if they are to succeed. Someone or some group must prepare the newsletter, call meetings, register new members, keep the accounts and plan ahead. Networks should not be seen as permanent structures. Once they have fulfilled a need they should be allowed to die, and their death may well give birth to a new and different network.

4.4   Making changes in educational policies and practices

The ways by which individuals and organizations can make changes in educational policies and practices vary from institution to institution and from country to country. But the basic step-by-step process will be similar. First, the situation must be analyzed and the problem identified. Next, various strategies for implementing change must be considered and suitable ones chosen. At this stage community support should be assessed and a public relations program initiated if necessary. Then the program of change must be planned, implemented and, in time, evaluated. Teachers, because of their expertise, should be a part of that change-making process. However, as Nisbet and Broadfoot point out

> The influence teachers can have on policy and practice at any one level of educational activity, be it classroom, school, local authority or national, depends on a number of inter-related factors: 1) whether the decision making structures at each level are authoritarian or democratic; 2) the extent to which teachers as individuals or as a group possess skills in professional, social and political decision making and have knowledge of the system and policies they wish to influence; 3) the amount of time available to the teacher to participate; 4) the amount of back-up help received by teachers in terms of curriculum resources, in-service training, consultations with advisers and colleagues and advice from professional associations.[10]

Few people have been trained in the art of making changes in educational practices. It is one of those skills one learns on the job. The following axioms have been tested by practicing teachers and found to be helpful. However, not all axioms are applicable to all individuals or all organizations. Readers must choose those which appear to offer some chance of success in making changes. The 'you' addressed in the axioms may be an individual or an organization or both; that is, whatever the situation demands.

1. *Be quite clear in your own mind what the problem is that needs to be addressed and what needs to be done.*

If you are not clear in your own mind what the heart of the problem is and what needs to be done about it, you will never convince anyone that you are anything more than a perennial grumbler.

The problem may be one of two kinds: educational or societal. But each, of course, affects the other. Educational problems spill over and become societal issues, and societal problems often demand the attention of educational institutions. Educational problems concern such matters as poor organization or administration of a program, a lack of services to students, an outdated curriculum, poor teacher morale, or inadequately prepared teachers. Societal problems center on groups which are not being adequately served, or on discrimination, or on funding cutbacks, or on a lack of public awareness regarding the difficulties faced by minority groups. Because modern-day societies are complex networks of power and powerlessness, of dependency and independency, of ignorance and knowledge, few problems are simple and straightforward. It takes time to reach the essence of the problem and to imagine possible solutions, but it will be time well spent. You cannot explain to others what you cannot explain to yourself.

2. *Collect the facts and figures that you need to prove that you have a case.*

The phrase 'a lot of people' does not carry nearly as much weight as 'fifty' or 'five thousand' or whatever number fits the situation. Figures are often available if you search long enough and ask enough questions of enough people. If figures are not available, then perhaps this 'fact" that no one has cared enough to find out, for example, the second language needs of pre-school children, ought to be made public to show up the lack of concern for those who cannot help themselves. Facts, or the established absence of facts, give strength to a brief.

University and public libraries may have some of the answers. If they don't, you may have to send out your own questionnaire or conduct interviews with possible informants. Facts which are hard to refute provide a good foundation for actions which may follow.

3. *Decide on your four or five major priorities – then pick the one you think you can be reasonably sure of completing successfully and get on with it quickly.*

The nature of some problems is that they need to be addressed from a number of standpoints if real change is to occur, but it is unlikely that everything can be done simultaneously. The proposed actions should be set in order of priority; that is, those that are most important should be listed at the top. However, for a variety of reasons, these items may not be the ones that will produce quick visible results. Nothing succeeds like success, so choose an item with a lower priority that you know you can succeed with and work on it. When you have been successful once, people start to take notice of you. The news will spread that you don't just talk – you act! Once you have established a positive reputation, you can get on with some of the long-term more important items on your priority list.

4. *Gather a few like-minded people around you.*

Your collective enthusiasm will attract others. Many successful movements of the past, whether social, political, religious or educational were rooted in the beliefs and actions of a mere handful of people who refused to be defeated. But choose wisely! There are some people who flit from cause to cause like grasshoppers. Eschew them! Seek out sincere people from education or from the community, people who are prepared to listen as well as talk, to give as well as get. Seek people from a variety of backgrounds so that their input adds new dimensions both to the problem and to its solution. Seek quality not quantity initially; quantity will take care of itself when the bandwagon starts rolling.

5. *Encourage outsiders to meet your students and to see what goes on in your classroom.*

Don't let language teaching become a 'mystery cult' in your institution. Administrators and other teachers, as well as members of the local community, need to see for themselves what you are talking about when you say you want to make changes. You cannot expect people to support you when they really do not know who your students are and what their needs are. Show them. If possible, let them experience the problem at first hand by meeting those who are affected.

6. *Get to know some government officials, municipal, regional and national, on a personal basis.*

There are many sincere and dedicated civil servants who experience the same joys and frustrations as teachers do in trying to change the world. When you know them, you will find they will give you good counsel and win your respect. Influential people in ministries of education and other government departments are part of the power network. They can affect policy-making decisions and without the support of some of them you may expend much energy for sparse results. Establishing acquaintanceships with officials gives access to the power structure and information on how it can be used.

7. *Take an active part in local politics.*

You don't have to be elected to a position but do know what is going on in your local community. Be an informed voter and be ready to inform others. Serve on a community-based committee and become known. You need to become part of the network if you are going to get the support of others, and you need to know who the influential people are who can help you. You learn more about the game by playing it than by standing on the sidelines.

8. *Support your teachers' organization and be prepared to give it some time and to serve on a committee.*

The energy which fuels an organization comes from the individual members. If your organization has not done as much as you think it should have done, perhaps it is just short of member-energy. No organization can be effective in helping to make changes if it does not have sufficient people willing to take on part of the work.

9. *But remember that the individual is just as important as an organization – both have a role to play in making changes.*

Not everyone is an 'organization person'. Some are loners and work better on their own. There are many examples, even in today's complex world, of the power of the committed individual. But working alone may take more time and energy. One solution is to work on a particular piece of the problem, joining with others from time to time so that the whole does not get fragmented into too many parts.

10. *Make your organization truly representative – don't let cliques develop.*

A good mixture of people who represent different geographical regions, different types of institutions, different student bodies, and different levels of instruction will make the pinpointing of problems common to all much easier, allowing battle to be enjoined on a number of fronts simultaneously. Leaders of any organization must consciously recruit new people who will bring a fresh look at the situation, but as it takes time to orient them to what has gone before, it is often easier to stick with the old members and the old ways and to cold shoulder those who seek admittance. Periodic checks of lists of committee members will indicate whether the organization is renewing itself or whether the same tired and ageing people are simply changing seats.

11. *Advertise your organization and its cause.*

Send out brochures. Get on the media. Remember that 'out of sight' does mean 'out of mind'. If no one knows that your organization exists, it has only itself to blame if it is not consulted on issues in education or in the community that affect it.

12. *Join hands with organizations in the local community that have similar interests.*

A good communications network can ensure that organizations work in support of each other and not at cross-purposes. There is strength in numbers and there is much to be gained from working cooperatively. Information is a vital resource. When community groups meet, information can be exchanged which may later be transformed into power. Coordination of efforts can also ensure that aspects of the problem are not overlooked or that two organizations do not expend energy unnecessarily by duplicating the work of the other.

13. *Join hands also with national and international organizations.*

Look wider than your local community. Be ready to speak with others on matters of national and international importance and to learn from their experience. We live in one world and what is occurring here today may already have occurred elsewhere and may be about to happen somewhere else. Matters of national and international concern get wider exposure in the media which may help your cause.

14. *Keep personally well informed on what is happening in your field locally, nationally and internationally; and as an organization keep your members well informed.*

Every language teacher is a public affairs representative for language teaching and must be ready to speak knowledgeably about the concerns and achievements in the field.

15. *Make sure you know which concerns come under the local government and which come under the national government.*

Kicking the football back and forth is an old game played by local and national politicians. Don't give them an excuse for a game by taking a request to the wrong group. But if they do play football with you, make sure there is a crowd (the public) watching. There is nothing like a wide-awake audience for keeping the players honest. After all, the audience pays the players' salaries! It sometimes takes time to track down who is responsible for what, but persistent questioning will eventually produce answers.

16. *Find a politician in power and another in opposition and cultivate them.*

Send them information, invite them to meet you, get on first-name terms with someone in their office, and then seek their support for your cause. Do not wait so long between the times you contact them that they have forgotten who you are and what changes you are seeking, but do not phone so often that you become a nuisance!

17. *Show these politicians what benefits they may reap from supporting your cause – votes? publicity?*

Politicians are busy people and need some pay-off for the time they give you. They need to get their names in the newspapers supporting something approved of by the community. Their future, after all, depends upon what their electors think of them.

18. *Ask questions* before *making accusations.*

You may be wrong. Asking a few simple but direct questions is an important component in the process of making changes. It is very easy to jump to a wrong conclusion after hearing or reading a media report. The media thrives on sensation and picks those elements of a story which provide sensation. Half-truths and distortions can be accepted as truths. The emotional response which follows can be damaging, particularly when it is later found to be based on misinformation. Unemotional questions posed to those who should know will elicit the kind of information on which a rational response can be based.

19. *Be professional in fact not in fiction.*

That is, be properly trained, if possible in connection with a university. Engage in classroom action research. Write articles dealing with your own expertise. Learn from the ever-increasing body of knowledge about language teaching and add to it. To be a professional, a person must be well acquainted with the body of knowledge in a particular discipline and must engage in professional activities. As status is often important in the process of making changes in education and society, language teachers must ensure that they measure up as professionals.

20. *Be prepared to be hurt.*

If you want to make changes in society, you will be vulnerable to personal attack. But remember – the hurt you will feel will probably be nothing compared to the hurt presently felt by those for whom change is desperately needed. Your colleagues may openly laugh at you or make comments about you behind your back. You may be criticized in the newspapers. But if you have prepared yourself properly by following some of the axioms suggested above, criticism will fall away and support will grow.

Some years ago most changes in education were handed down from the top. In recent years, changes have been wrought in other ways. Those planning changes should consider which of the following ways may be more productive in producing change. Various factors have to be taken into account – the participants, the time, place, and desired outcome.

1. Some people respond best to rational arguments. They appreciate receiving well-documented reports with clearly defined objectives and recommendations.
2. Some people need to have their hearts touched before their heads will become involved. They need to see and feel the problem before they can come to grips with it.
3. Some people are very wary of large-scale change and prefer to move small steps at a time. A large proposal will cause them to back off.
4. Some people do not act until they are placed under considerable pressure. They do not feel the special interest group is serious until confrontation takes place.
5. Some people like to negotiate this for that. It is as well to have something ready to give up.
6. Some people like to turn every issue into a political issue and enjoy the battles which ensue.
7. But others prefer a low-keyed slow-moving approach.

PERSONAL PRIORITIES AND MODES OF ACTION

In working with local communities, teachers must be aware of their own priorities in their professional and personal lives and of their preferred modes of action. The following questions are designed to help teachers decide on the possible nature of their involvement with the community:

1. What is your present involvement in and with the local community?
2. What are your professional ambitions? What position would you like to hold five years from now?
3. How much time can you give to working with the local community on community projects?
4. How can you involve the local community in your teaching situation? How can the community help you?
5. Do you like working with organizations or are you a loner?
6. What are your strengths and weaknesses in working with others?
7. What organization might you join that would help you achieve your personal and professional ambitions?
8. What status does that organization have in the community? Will the contacts you make be useful to you and your students?
9. What experiences have you had that the local community could draw on and use? What do you have to offer?
10. Which of the ideas contained in this chapter can you use in your situation?

Activities

1. What changes have occurred in emigration or immigration policies in your country that are having or will have an impact on language teaching? Prepare a short article for publication.
2. What current social policies in areas of human rights, employment opportunities, affirmative action, financial support, or access to information and counselling enhance or restrict language learning in your community? Bring together a group of experts for a panel discussion.
3. What minority language rights are encoded in law or unofficially sanctioned? What rights are denied to minority groups and with what results? Prepare a report.
4. How is language teaching contributing to equal employment opportunities for speakers of other languages? Describe a program sponsored jointly by an employer and an educational institution, or draw up a plan for such a program in your community.

5. Take a problem currently facing a group of language teachers in your community and thoroughly research it. Write up a brief with recommendations for action.
6. Examine the objectives of your local teachers' organization, its administration and power structure. Become familiar with its past performance on issues connected with language teaching and any policies it may have which affect language teaching.
7. Answer the questions under 'Personal priorities and modes of action' and decide on the kind of community involvement that suits your personality and goals.

5 Teaching English internationally

After examining reasons for the spread of English around the world, this chapter will focus on various issues related to teaching English internationally.

5.1 Overview

Since 1945 the number of jobs around the world for teachers of English has greatly increased as has the number of countries seeking the services of native speakers of English. It is possible now to have a fulltime career either teaching English as a foreign language or training non-native speakers to teach English in their own country.

Teaching languages internationally today presents new issues and new challenges. These relate not only to curriculum and program planning but also to the ethics and values which lie behind second language teaching, raising a number of fundamental questions regarding the manner in which language teachers should respond. The old paternalism or cultural imperialism of the past gave teachers a sense that what they did and the way in which they did it was, if not absolutely right, at least better than what was being done. That certainty has gone.

This chapter will start (5.2) by examining the reasons for the spread of English around the world. The next section (5.3) will consider some issues that arise when a foreign language and/or foreign teaching methods are exported and imported. The last section (5.4) will look at employment possibilities, and at problems that may face language teachers heading off on their first international assignment.

5.2 The spread of English

It has been estimated that approximately 300 million people speak English as their first language and an equal number as their second language.[1] This spread of English around the world began with the explorers of the sixteenth century and was carried on by merchants and missionaries. It was given further impetus by two major events: 1) British imperialism of the nineteenth century and 2) the technical and scientific superiority of the United States and Britain during the twentieth century. The nineteenth century was an era of geographic expansion by European nations who established colonies throughout Africa and Asia, imposing their languages, their religions, and their forms of government upon the defeated people. Britain was particularly successful in building up a large empire in all quarters of the globe so that it was said with pride that the sun never set on the British Empire. In its turn, the twentieth century brought advances in science and technology beyond the imagination of most people: the automobile, the aeroplane, radio, television, radar, computers, rockets, missiles, the atomic bomb and the H-bomb. Initially, many of the consumer items were mass produced in the United States and Britain and exported to countries who sought them, but gradually the developing countries began to establish their own industries giving further strength to the maintenance and spread of English through trade, science and technology.

Throughout history, many nations engaged in conquest and sub-jugation, in trade and commerce. Their languages were employed as languages of wider communication for some years, perhaps centuries, until finally they lost their dominance. Fishman, Cooper and Rosenbaum list nine factors which may affect the spread of a particular language, its use as an additional language, and its eventual acceptance as the mother tongue. These are paraphrased below:

1. *Military conquest.* Military conquest can result in the language of the conquerors becoming the language of the administration of the territory.
2. *Duration of military authority.* If the duration of the military authority extends over a long period of time, perhaps centuries, the language has time to take root.
3. *Linguistic diversity.* In multilingual areas, a unified administration promotes commercial, religious and political contacts among linguistically diverse people.
4. *Material benefits.* Learning a language of wider communication may result in material benefits.
5. *Urbanization.* Because towns tend to be more linguistically diverse and contain within them government agencies and better educational opportunities, they tend to serve as the loci for the spread of an additional language.
6. *Economic development.* Economic underdevelopment may promote reliance upon a language of wider communication for functions that might be satisfied by a local language in a more developed economy.
7. *Educational development.* Economic development may require that a language of wider communication is taught in the schools.
8. *Religious composition.* Areas of ethnic and religious diversity (which may also be underdeveloped economically and educationally) tend to promote the spread of a lingua franca.

9. *Political affiliation.* The position of a country in relation to the superpowers may be reflected in the language used as the medium of instruction in the schools or taught as a subject.[2]

In an attempt to discover which of these nine factors were useful in predicting how widely English is used in the educational systems of 102 countries, Fishman et al. collected information covering demographic, economic, educational and other factors. In none of the countries studied was English the mother tongue of a substantial part of the population. The best predictor of the spread of English as an additional language was, not surprisingly, found to be the former Anglophone colonial status of the country, followed by linguistic diversity, religious composition, and educational and economic development.[3] That linguistic diversity and religious composition rate high as predictors can perhaps be explained by the need for a lingua franca in areas where a sense of unity fostered through the use of a common language can encourage economic and educational development.

The researchers have a caveat for their readers:

> To say that English is spreading around the world as a function of the combination of particular variables is a summarizing statement, based on the effects of innumerable human interactions and motivations. Individuals, not countries, learn English as an additional language. An individual learns English, moreover, not because of abstractions such as linguistic diversity or international trade balances but because the knowledge of English helps him to communicate in contexts in which, for economic or educational or emotional reasons, he wants to communicate and because the opportunity to learn English is available to him.[4]

Peter Strevens points out that three kinds of expansion of English need to be recognized: number of users of English; range of uses of English; number of local forms of English.[5] These categories will act as organizers for what follows.

Number of users of English

All over the world students in primary and secondary schools, in colleges and universities are struggling to learn English. A sampling of those countries which have large enrolments in English-medium classes or English subject classes is as follows: India, Philippines, USSR, People's Republic of China, Hong Kong, Japan, Nigeria, West Germany, France, Mexico, Kenya, Ghana, Brazil, Thailand. While the number of users of English has expanded during the past decades of this century, predictions for the continued spread of English are guarded. Two factors may slow it down: 1) the growing influence of non-English-speaking superpowers such as Russia and China whose languages will undoubtedly be exported with their influence; and 2) the movement of some ex-colonies away from regarding English as a second language and towards regarding it as a foreign language (e.g. Malaysia), thus limiting its status while increasing the status of an indigenous language.

Human language serves two functions: 1) the communicative function, that of providing for the conveyance of meaning between social groups; and 2) the identifying function, that of expressing and preserving intragroup identity.[6] With regard to the former, H. G. Widdowson questions whether it is possible to strip a language down to the bare essentials needed for impersonal reference and communication without depriving it of its potential for creativity and change. With regard to the latter, Widdowson sees as 'a dangerous ideal' the views of 'some fundamentalist visionaries who interpret the brotherhood of man quite literally as a realizable ideal and who see all societies as constituents of one vast and homogeneous social group with English as their means of identification, all subscribing to the same set of beliefs, all recognizing the same canons of acceptable behavior'. He also questions the need to promote English further in either of these areas, it being already widely used in academic and occupational endeavors. 'It would seem to be more sensible,' he writes, 'to support the role that English has already acquired than to spend time and effort dreaming up ways of making it more international than it already is.'[7]

Range of uses of English

The spread of English has naturally resulted in the creation of terminology to describe the teaching and learning of English as an additional language. While the acronyms ESL (English as a Second Language) and EFL (English as a Foreign Language) give some indication as to whether the language is being learned in an English-speaking milieu for the purpose of day-to-day communication or whether it is being learned in a non-English-speaking milieu for more restricted purposes, these terms do not indicate what those purposes might be. Participants at a conference in Honolulu in 1978 felt that a distinction had to be made between two uses of English: 1) English for international (i.e. external) purposes as represented by a country like Japan; and 2) English for intranational (i.e. internal) purposes as represented by a country like India.[8] Hence, a new acronym came into being: EIIL – English as an International/Intranational Language. (For a list of the various acronyms used in second language teaching, see Appendix B.)

But while that term may describe the uses to which nations put English, it does not describe the uses to which individuals put English, and hence their reasons for learning the language. Two studies carried out, one in Israel and the other in India, Thailand and the Republic of

Singapore, give some clues as to the uses to which students are putting or expect to put English. The first study by Robert L. Cooper and Fern Seckbach looked at the economic incentives for learning English in Israel. They tabulated the language requirements specified in job advertisements in the daily newspapers and concluded that 'economic considerations do indeed play an important role in promoting the spread and maintenance of languages of wider communication'. They pointed out that language learning was no longer just for the elite.

> The importance of English for white-collar jobs suggests that a strong incentive to learn English exists among ordinary citizens, persons who are not likely to continue their formal education beyond high school and who will thus not need English for post-secondary school studies. Thus for many of the students who do not plan to continue their studies beyond high school, English can be viewed with some justification as a bread-and butter skill, much as is shorthand, typing and bookkeeping.[9]

In a second study by Willard D. Shaw, students from the three large Asian cities of Hyderabad, India, and Bangkok, Thailand, and Singapore, the Republic of Singapore, were asked to rate from a list of twenty-five statements their reasons for learning English. The most frequently given reasons by all students were the following:

(a) I studied English because I will need it for my work.
(b) I studied English so I could talk to native speakers of English for business/educational reasons.
(c) I studied English so I could talk to other foreigners for business/educational reasons.
(d) I studied English because it is required in our system.
(e) I studied English because I believe that a knowledge of another language will make me a better person.

In addition, (f) the Singaporeans claimed that it was necessary to study English in order to get a good job. (g) Students from Hyderabd felt that English provided them with a link to other people in India whose language they did not speak. (h) The Thais saw English as useful for general work purposes.

The four reasons that ranked at the bottom for all three groups of students were these:

(i) I studied English because I like the countries in which English is spoken.
(j) I studied English because I like the people who are native speakers of English.
(k) I studied English because I plan to travel to non-English-speaking (sic) countries someday for my work.
(l) I studied English because it will help me to think and behave as native speakers do.[10]

These results make it clear that the students were learning English for instrumental purposes; that is, to help them in their careers. They were not learning English for integrative purposes; that is, in order to become integrated members of the English-speaking community.

The range of uses to which English is put obviously varies somewhat from country to country and changes as the internal and external circumstances of the country change.

Number of local forms of English

Any study of the spread of English is simultaneously a study of the history of England. From that country the language was carried to North America, Southwest Asia, Africa and Australasia with the result that today there are many local forms of English (LFEs). The two main branches of English are the British English branch which embraces the varieties of English as spoken in Great Britain, the West Indies, Africa, India, Southwest Asia and Australasia; and the American branch covering the United States and Canada. Standard English is the dialect used and understood by educated people all over the world. It is the dialect in which literature is written and commented on, and is considered by many people to be the most appropriate model to use in teaching English as a second or foreign language.

However, because languages change with time and in contact with other languages, a number of local forms of English have grown up, such that within a large country like India one LFE may be almost incomprehensible to speakers of another LFE. While both LFEs have evolved from the same stock, circumstances have caused them to evolve differently. Some of them may have begun as pidgins and developed into creoles by serving the needs of traders; others may have been established as the national language through the administration of a colonial government. There is, therefore, a hierarchy of Englishes: pidgins, creoles, local, regional and national Englishes, as well as standard English for international purposes.

The question facing teachers of English is whether standard English is always the best model to employ. Where English is used solely as an international language, it undoubtedly is; but where English is used as an intranational language, an LFE may be the preferred model, perhaps in place of standard English, perhaps in addition to it.

Joshua Fishman, one of the leading scholars studying the spread of English, provides a good summary statement for this section:

> A host of factors have come together to foster the spread of English
> as a lingua franca in this very day and age when the number of
> independent countries is larger than it has ever been before in
> recorded history. However, notwithstanding the proliferation of

polities – each gravitating toward one or more indigenous official/national languages – the number of 'international' people has also kept growing, as a result of growth in the number of foreign technological experts, more cosmopolitan local indigenous elites, business representatives of Anglophone commercial enterprises, and expatriate students and residents, as well as because of the vastly increased tide of tourism. In city after city throughout the world these internationals constitute a speech community (superimposed upon innumerable smaller networks that are often based on divergent mother tongues) precisely because English is their lingua franca – as revealed in shops, clubs, restaurants, theaters, and concerts and by parties, publications, and mass media preferences the world over, far above and beyond the requirements of industry, technology, and (inter)governmental relations from which the international use of English initially stems. Indeed, probably never before has so much of the world been so accessible via a single language, as well as via one whose volume and value at a reasonable 'standardized' level is sufficiently great and sufficiently monitored to obviate any danger of its fragmentation into a variety of new languages.[11]

5.3 Exporting English

Second language teaching is not a commodity that can be exported as if it were an object – it is a process which affects people's lives. There are therefore ethical and professional considerations to be taken into account, and responsibilities to be assumed. In this section we will look first at the ethics of teaching internationally, then at the problems of exporting methodologies, and finally at international collaboration.

Ethics

EFL TEACHER REQUIRED TO DESIGN LANGUAGE PROGRAM FOR APPRENTICE INTERROGATORS. THESE STUDENTS REQUIRE FLUENT COMMAND OF COLLOQUIAL ENGLISH IN ORDER TO EFFECTIVELY QUESTION, INTIMIDATE AND THREATEN POLITICAL PRISONERS, AS WELL AS ACADEMIC LANGUAGE WITH WHICH TO STUDY AND RECEIVE TRAINING IN UP-TO-DATE TORTURE TECHNIQUES. CANDIDATES SHOULD BE EXPERIENCED IN THE COMMUNICATIVE APPROACH.[12]

As David Lee Jackson points out, 'A job such as this fills our hearts with horror and repugnance – nearly all of us have a powerful intuitive feeling that it is wrong.' But this extreme case (invented by Jackson for the purpose of illustrating his point) is not likely to confront teachers of English. They may, however, find themselves in situations where the consequences of their work may be, at best, uncertain, and, at worst, negative. 'They may be teaching the elite members of a repressive right-wing regime, or they may be teaching nuclear physicists in an aggressive, unstable socialist dictatorship. In many cases they do not know exactly who they are teaching or what their students will do with their English skills.'[13]

Educating people has political consequences. Information is power. Literacy, which is the key to information, is therefore power. Knowledge of a language of wider communication gives access to additional information, and therefore to power. Those who teach provide those who learn with options and opportunities that they can exercise, if they wish, within the political arena of their country. This political aspect of education raises a number of moral and ethical questions for teachers going abroad, questions which they can only answer in the context of the country to which they are going, the relationship of their own country to the country in which they will be teaching, and their own personal value system.

The ten questions which follow have all been raised before in various contexts and have resulted in various answers. Often the search for that elusive, definitive answer simply raises more issues. In the questions below the term 'foreign expert', which is now fairly widely used, has been substituted for 'language teacher'. While this term has the advantage of emphasizing that the language teacher is not familiar with the local scene – he/she is 'foreign' – , it has the disadvantage of suggesting that the language teacher is omniscient – knows everything –, and that is a very dangerous assumption. These questions are intended to be springboards for thought for teachers preparing to teach internationally for the first time.

1. Will the teaching act uphold or run counter to the UN Declaration of Human Rights, the Convention against Discrimination in Education, or the Declaration of the Rights of the Child?
2. Will the teaching act, by increasing the opportunities for some, result in oppression for others? Does one group advance at the expense of another?
3. When a foreign expert believes that the knowledge gained by the students may result in increased oppression for others, should he/she refuse to teach, or should he/she adopt the attitude that, as someone will do it, better me than him/her?
4. Should foreign experts consciously and deliberately teach their students their rights as workers or citizens if they believe these are withheld from them?
5. Should foreign experts impose their values on their students when they sincerely believe their values are better than those currently being practiced?

6. Should foreign experts play a subversive role, that of teaching students how to make changes in the systems which control them?
7. Does the presence of foreign experts in countries which have oppressive regimes automatically suggest that the regime is condoned by the supplying country? If so, should foreign experts be there?
8. If the difference between the working conditions and salaries of the local teachers and those of the foreign experts is very great, how should the foreign experts react?
9. Should foreign experts judge another society, its values, customs and traditions, or should they simply accept what is?
10. Do foreign experts have the right to interfere in the internal politics of another country?

Methodology

In chapter 3 under 'Families', the case was made that when the teaching style of the teacher does not mesh with the learning style of the student frustration and discord result. Methodologies make certain assumptions about how students learn or how, in the view of the teacher, they should learn, and therefore how teachers should teach. Many new methodologies have arisen in the English-speaking countries during the last few decades following the breakdown of the dominance of the audio-lingual method: cognitive-code, 'silent way', counselling–learning, total physical response, 'suggestopedia', and the communicative approach. The question raised by Gloria Paulik Sampson in her article entitled 'Exporting language teaching methods from Canada to China' is: should foreign methods be used to teach foreign languages?[14] She posits the following three arguments against the automatic export and import of foreign teaching methods.

I. THE FALLACY OF THE UNIDIMENSIONALITY OF DEVELOPMENT

Because developed nations export finished products representing high technology, it is assumed by some that whatever else they export, including ideas, is also highly developed. This, Sampson claims, is a fallacy. She cites as an example Nazi Germany of the 1930s, a country highly developed technologically, but whose ideas regarding society and education were hardly of the same calibre. Sampson suggests that ESL/EFL teachers should not make the mistake of labeling a country with the unidimensional label of advanced or backward. A country which is well-developed technologically may not be well-developed socially. This leads to her next issue.

2. SIMILARITIES AND DIFFERENCES BETWEEN SCIENTIFIC AND EDUCATIONAL THEORIES

Sampson points out that while scientific theory is value-free, educational theory, because it is based in a particular view of human nature and the socialization process, is value-laden.

> These observations lead to the conclusion that an educational theory shares the attributes of a political or moral theory; one speaks of 'good' or 'bad' educational practices. And, of course, what is good or bad is always dependent on particular circumstances. What is good educational practice in Canada might be construed as bad in China, and vice versa.

Different countries have different theories of education. 'An educational theory is used to judge the findings of scientific theories and assess whether particular scientific findings can in fact be applied to specific school settings without harming human beings.' Language teachers should be clear in their own minds whether the methodology they propose to use overseas has a scientific or an educational base.

3. TECHNOCRATIC IMPERIALISM

This, Sampson says, 'is a form of export of intellectual goods which claims to be value-free and therefore the goods are deemed appropriate for all countries'. Countries which do not accept these goods are accused of being non-scientific. But every method contains an inherent set of principles, assumptions and therefore values. The Chinese, for example, have been criticized for their excessive focus on memorization, a process abhorred by many native-speaking ESL/EFL teachers. But in the Chinese educational system both the teacher and the text are models for the learners, and one way to internalize the textual model is to memorize it.

> In short, the text, the written word, has a value and has consequences in China far beyond anything North Americans can imagine in their own mercantile cultures. From the Chinese perspective, memorization is far from being an easy cop-out or a release from thinking. It is considered the initial step in assimilating a lesson. To know a text by memory first of all means that the text is important to the learner. To be able to recapitulate that text by memory means that the learner can play with it in his mind at will. Only after the text is internalized through memorization can it be considered the learner's text as well. So, memorization becomes an important first response to a text in a society which takes the written word seriously.[15]

When the 'silent way' was in vogue, some ESL/EFL teachers interested in studying the new method at firsthand became students learning a new language through this approach. For some the change from the teacher-centered audio-lingual classroom to the learner-centered classroom was enjoyable and beneficial: they learned the language and incorporated some of the teaching techniques in their own classroom practices. For others the change was abhorrent: they resisted the new method, learned little of the language, and incorporated none of the techniques in their teaching. The lesson to be learned is that methods and techniques should be fitted to the students; students should not be forced into one predetermined teaching/learning mould. That does not mean teachers should not introduce any new methods or techniques – far from it. But they should first come to an understanding of why a particular method is used and how effective it is in attaining the goals of the program. Visitors to China are often very surprised at the high quality of English spoken by students who have employed rote memorization. EFL teachers should study the educational system – its values, structure, and goals – and the social and economic systems; and they should consult with local teachers and try to see the situation through their eyes before launching into a program of change which may be both harmful and ineffective. It is better to make haste slowly! What works in the United States, Britain, Canada and Australia may not work in China, Nigeria, Thailand or Saudi Arabia, and vice versa. The teacher who wrote home that her students were 'freaked out' by her teaching methods was still learning the meaning of cultural imperialism. Care should be taken at all times to ensure that the methods and techniques used enhance learning and create positive classroom atmospheres.

International collaboration

The dropping of the atomic bomb on Japan in 1945 jolted the world into some modicum of sense. Now that people had the capacity to destroy themselves totally, it was time to start talking to each other before they ended it all. With the old League of Nations lying shamefully dead, hope rested with the new United Nations Organization which has proved, unfortunately, to be far from united. Over the years the United Nations has spawned a variety of sub-groups responsible for particular areas of human activity such as the World Health Organization (WHO) and the Food and Agriculture Organization (FAO).

There are a number of international organizations, some of which are part of the United Nations Organization, which directly or indirectly affect the teaching of English internationally by supplying funds and human and material resources for educational and economic development in developing countries. The better known of these are
United Nations Educational, Scientific and Cultural Organization
United Nations International Child Emergency Fund

Organization for Economic Cooperation and Development
The International Bureau of Education
The International Institute for Educational Planning
The World Organization for Early Childhood Education
The International Federation of Children's Communities
The World Bank
The Council of Europe

A step down from international organizations are the national groups such as the British Council which has played an important role in training and supplying EFL teachers, both native and non-native speakers of English, and in developing programs and materials. In the United States over the years the State Department's Bureau of Educational Policy and Cultural Affairs, the Agency for International Development, and the United States Information Agency have all been involved with aspects of teaching English internationally. Similarly Canada and Australia, through government sponsored programs have contributed to the spread and improvement of EFL programs. (For a list of agencies and organizations concerned with teaching English as a second/foreign language, consult Appendix C.)

Some universities in the English-speaking world are working closely with universities in other parts of the world – sometimes known as 'twinning'. Members of the two faculties engage in collaborative research, and exchange places to enable them to study in the other country. Professors and students involved in theoretical and practical aspects of language teaching have been able to take advantage of these inter-university programs. Less-qualified people may get an opportunity to teach languages (or other subjects) through such programs as the Peace Corps (United States), VSO (Britain), and CUSO (Canada). In addition, international and national teachers' organizations have provided resources, human and material, to assist in the upgrading of English language teaching.

5.4 International employment possibilities and problems

TYPES OF JOBS

At the university level, instructors may be hired to perform the following functions:
– teaching theoretical aspects of second language instruction such as linguistics, sociolinguistics, or psycholinguistics;
– training EFL teachers through instruction in methodology and through observation and practice teaching;

– teaching English to graduate and undergraduate students who are studying to become EFL teachers or translators, or who plan to study abroad, or who require limited proficiency in a foreign language to satisfy degree requirements.

In addition, public/state schools and private language schools hire native speakers of English to teach a variety of courses, as do some commercial firms whose business depends on some employees having a reasonable command of English. Increasingly, as more students are going to English-speaking countries to study, courses are being developed specifically for the overseas-bound student. Instructors are also hired to develop programs, materials, and testing instruments, and not necessarily to teach.

QUALIFICATIONS

Universities usually demand a Ph.D or Master's degree in English as a second/foreign language or in linguistics. Below this level, qualifications sought depend on the prestige of the institution and its ability to pay. Reputable institutions usually look for the following: 1) a baccalaureate or higher degree; 2) TESL/TEFL training; and 3) native-like command of English.

OBTAINING A JOB

There is no one way to obtain an international teaching position. The following are the normal methods:
– by contacting national organizations within one's own country that are responsible for placing teachers abroad;
– by approaching one or more persons who have taught or lived elsewhere and finding out how jobs are obtained in a particular country;
– by subscribing to journals and newsletters that advertise jobs in other countries;
– by contacting the embassy or consulate of the country one is interested in teaching in for information on how to obtain a job and the legalities of working there;
– by visiting the country of one's choice and making contact with institutions that hire EFL teachers.

CONTRACTS

Prospective employees should read the large and fine print of the contract slowly, carefully and thoughtfully a number of times before signing. Contracts with international and national agencies are usually fairly standard and trustworthy, but contracts with private language

schools should be very well checked out. Before accepting a position teachers should know
- the hours they will be expected to work each day;
- the number of days they will be expected to work each week (not all countries are on a five day week);
- the duties they will be expected to perform;
- the statutory and other holidays they will receive;
- the pay;
- the additional benefits they will receive, e.g. medical insurance;
- the conditions under which their fares will be paid over and back;
- whether or not their families can accompany them;
- whether or not living accommodation is provided, and if so what it consists of;
- whether or not the contract is renewable.

PROBLEMS WHICH MAY BE ENCOUNTERED

Not everyone is suited to teaching in another part of the world. For some, the initial excitement turns to frustration and despair because the living and working conditions fall far short of what the new arrival expected and perhaps short of what is reasonable. Teachers should be prepared to suffer culture shock and should therefore give themselves time to adjust before making final judgments on their situation. While the challenges may, on occasions, seem insurmountable, time and patience, coupled with an effort to understand, often reduces them to manageable proportions. A sense of humor is imperative! The following are areas where teachers have, in the past, encountered problems:
- Classes are larger than they have been used to.
- Print and non-print materials are in short supply and out-of-date, and audio-visual aids, including blackboards, are limited.
- A different methodology is used.
- The teaching load is heavier than at home.
- The new teacher (as the foreign expert) is required immediately to design and teach new courses with little preliminary warning.
- There are incessant demands for the foreign expert to give talks, conduct workshops and attend meetings in his/her 'free time'.
- Contact with the local people, teachers and students, out of working hours is limited and loneliness seems to be the alternative, or
- Privacy is non-existent as visitors eager to meet the foreign expert are constantly dropping by.
- Hoped for extensive travel within the country does not materialize.
- Keeping healthy takes much longer than at home; general hygiene and the preparation of food assumes greater importance.
- Medical attention may not be readily available.
- The weather in the rainy season can be awful and the bugs horrendous!

But the benefits of spending a year or more in another country are, in most instances, greater than the problems encountered. To become familiar with another language and another culture is a broadening experience for which there is no substitute.

Activities

1. Expand on any one of the three categories, number of users of English, range of uses of English, or number of local forms of English, with respect to a particular country or region.
2. Write a report on the history and contribution of a national or international organization in the field of second language teaching.
3. Research the teaching of English as a foreign language in a country of your choice. Describe the history and goals of the program(s) and the involvement of foreign experts.
4. Organize a panel of returned foreign experts and get their views on teaching internationally.
5. Interview foreign students who are studying in your country on the nature and efficacy of the second language programs in their homeland.
6. Respond to one or more of the questions posed in the section on 'Ethics', pp. 121–2.

6 Predicting the future in language teaching

This chapter will look at ways in which language teachers can predict what the future may hold in order that they can play some part in moulding it.

6.1 Overview

While we cannot predict the future with any certainty (indeed, we cannot study a future which has not come but only ideas about a future which may be), that should not deter us from describing possible alternative futures and working towards the most desirable. To refuse to make any attempt to influence what may happen is social and educational suicide. The future is not fixed or predetermined. There are alternatives from which people can choose and, having chosen, can seek to implement. Decisions which are made or are not made today will affect the course of events five, ten or fifty years ahead, just as decisions made or not made five, ten or fifty years ago are affecting us today. The process of predicting the future in language teaching is a first step in affecting the future of language teaching.

T. S. Eliot wrote:

> Time present and time past
> Are both perhaps present in time future,
> And time future contained in time past.
> ('Burnt Norton')

Predicting the future with a reasonable promise of accuracy demands two kinds of knowledge: a knowledge of time past and a knowledge of time present, for both are contained in time future. As the collection and analysis of this data is beyond the ability of one person, the creation of a 'think-tank' of concerned educators and community leaders and workers can spread the work while bringing different viewpoints and experiences to bear on the difficult task of predicting the future. This chapter will look at (6.2) time past, (6.3) time present, and (6.4) time future in the context of second language teaching.

6.2 Time past

The future is rooted in the past. As Coleridge said, 'If men could learn from history, what lessons it might teach us.' The experiences of this century alone have much to teach us about the causes of mass migration of people (war, poverty, unstable economic systems, unacceptable political regimes, religious oppression), about how to work with governments, about the mercurial changes in public attitudes towards education or minority groups, about the administration of large institutions, about the role and efficacy of pressure groups, and about the need for constant vigilance that the rights of those who cannot speak for themselves are safeguarded.

Before they attempt to predict the future of language teaching, forecasters must be familiar with three histories:

1. *The history of language teaching.* Forecasters must be acquainted with the various approaches to language teaching that have developed over the years and the research, assumptions and principles which underlie those approaches.
2. *The history of the development of local language teaching programs.* Forecasters must know how and why local language programs were developed and what contributed to their success or failure. They must consider the degree to which the local community effectively played its three roles of beneficiary, resource and control in relation to language teaching.
3. *The history of local and world events which have affected language teaching.* Forecasters must identify local and world events which have affected what languages have been taught to which students in the community for what purposes.

Information gathered on these three histories will act as a backdrop to what is occurring right now.

6.3 Time present

In collecting data on the present, forecasters have to decide what is relevant to the language-teaching situation under review. For example, data on immigration is highly relevant to ESL teachers and to some heritage language teachers and perhaps bilingual education teachers; it is far less relevant to modern language teachers.

The following list may contain some topics relevant to some language-teaching situations, but forecasters will have to tease out for themselves those topics on which information is vital in understanding the present in order to predict the future:

– emigration and/or immigration statistics;
– demographic studies showing areas where certain languages predominate;

- statistics giving the numbers of people speaking specific languages in their homes;
- the state of the economies of other countries and of the world economy;
- local and national education policies;
- national policies affecting official and non-official languages;
- language policies in other countries;
- major world languages;
- statistics on how many students are studying particular languages;
- language programs currently offered at local institutions and their effectiveness;
- policy statements issued by any organization, local, national, or international, which is concerned in some way with language teaching.

When relevant data has been collected, the forecasters are ready to consider the future.

6.4 Time future

Before considering how to predict the future, it is necessary to clarify certain terms, as, by doing so, various options become more apparent. The following will be identified: trends, projections, forecasts, predictions, and scenarios.

Trends

John Naisbitt in his book *Megatrends* maintains that 'trends are bottom-up, fads are top-down';[1] that is, trends begin locally at the grassroots level and spread horizontally and vertically while fads are imposed from the top. Trends may take longer to be accepted but they may well last longer because they have the support of a community which has approved the trend and passed it on. A trend which has become established in language teaching is English for Special/Specific Purposes which grew in response to a need and spread widely. Naisbitt writes: 'Trends, like horses, are easier to ride in the direction they are already going. When you make a decision that is compatible with the overarching trend, the trend helps you along. You may decide to buck the trend, but it is still helpful to know it is there.'[2] Forecasters must distinguish between trends which may last and fads which may die.

Projections

Projections take established data and from it make an extrapolation into the future. If the parents of 500 kindergarten children indicate that they are committed to bilingual education for their children, by allowing for dropouts administrators can extrapolate how many bilingual education teachers will be needed to service those children at various grade levels.

Forecasts

A weather forecaster establishes what weather events are possible and assigns a degree of probability to each, for example, that there is a 20, 50 or 100 percent chance of rain. A language-teaching forecaster similarly establishes what events are possible and what degree of probability should be assigned to each.

Predictions

Predictions are firmer than forecasts. Having examined a number of factors, the predictor is able to say with a high degree of certainty what specific event may occur. When immigration doubles in one year, one can predict that the schools will feel the impact in proportion to the numbers and ages of the children admitted and the languages they speak.

Scenarios

Scenarios explore what may possibly happen by describing hypothetical sequences of events along the lines of 'If this happens, then this may follow as a result.' Scenario writing takes into account all available relevant data from the past and present, along with projections, forecasts and predictions, human behavior and natural laws. Although scenario writing entails imagination, the product outlined must be plausible. Often three scenarios will be presented: the best, the worst, and the most likely. For example, in times of financial restraint, funding for language programs may be reduced. For a particular program the 'best' scenario might show no cuts but no growth. The 'worst' scenario might show the program abolished. The 'most likely' might show the basic program left intact with cuts in some peripheral areas. If the 'worst' scenario is also the 'most likely' scenario, the program may be in serious difficulty unless some action can be taken to change the sequence of events.

It is only by projecting, forecasting, predicting, or writing scenarios that language teachers can become aware of what the future may hold and therefore what kind of decisions they may have to make in order to create an optimistic future for themselves and their students. The information collected on past history and present conditions will form two parts of the data used in predicting the future, but a third and equally important part will be a consideration of identifiable trends in a variety of areas which have the capacity to affect language teaching directly or indirectly. The following trends should be considered:

POPULATION

Populations are likely to increase in developing countries and remain static or decrease in developed countries. The proportion of young people to old will increase in developing countries and decrease in developed countries.
– Will your community have a shortfall or a surplus of people? Will this trigger immigration or emigration? Will these immigrants require language training?

URBANIZATION

Cities will probably continue to grow in number and in size attracting people from rural areas.
– Will these migrants require language training along with literacy or vocational training?

INDUSTRIALIZATION

Third-world countries will continue to build primary and secondary industries.
– Will the growth of industry require that students continue to study overseas to acquire new skills and that foreign experts travel abroad to teach new skills? Will language training be a part of the orientation of both groups and will it take place in your community?

SCIENCE AND TECHNOLOGY

Knowledge in these areas will continue to be created at a fast rate.
– How will the results of ongoing research, such as brain research, or high technology, such as computers, affect language teaching and how soon?

SPREAD OF LANGUAGES

The current position of English as the major world language may be challenged if the balance of political or commercial power shifts elsewhere.
– What major languages will be needed in the years ahead by people in your community working in some area of international trade or politics?

LANGUAGE TEACHING

Language teaching will continue to create new methods, approaches and techniques as it absorbs new knowledge from related disciplines.

– What institution, city or region is a trend-setter in language teaching? What are people there currently doing or saying? What topics are currently under discussion in reputable language journals? How do these topics relate to language teaching in your community?

CULTURAL PLURALISM

Perhaps in the distant future the world may become more racially homogeneous as intermarrying becomes more acceptable. In the meantime, cultural pluralism (the acceptance and appreciation of different cultures) is in its infancy and will need nurturing if it is to survive and grow to maturity.

– How strong is the desire in your community to teach or maintain heritage languages? How well would bilingual education be accepted? What can be done to create cultural and linguistic harmony in your community through language teaching?

RELIGION

The search for acceptable value systems and for personal philosophies will continue even though the old formal religious institutions may decline.

– Will the desire for religious freedom result in the establishment of more value or religious schools perhaps giving instruction in a non-official language? Will religious oppression continue to fill refugee camps with families who seek the right to worship. in their own way and in their own language, perhaps in your community?

POLITICAL DISSENSION

There is nothing to suggest that political dissension is going to stop overnight. There are too many 'isms' – capitalism, communism, socialism, conservatism, liberalism, fascism, totalitarianism – which arouse strong feelings and militant actions, making consensus impossible.

– What events are taking place elsewhere in the world that may trigger another political refugee movement? Will your community play host to political refugees?

WEALTH

Wealth will continue to be unequally distributed.

– Will the search for economic security continue to result in the migration of people from one part of the world to another? Will your community receive speakers of other languages looking for jobs?

POWER

The struggle for power will continue at all levels, locally, nationally, and internationally. The pendulum will probably continue to swing back and forth between centralization and decentralization until equilibrium is reached, which will not be in our lifetime!
– What organizational changes are taking place in your local institution(s) that may have an impact on language teaching? Does the power base in your local community show signs of shifting, if so, with what possible effects on language teaching?

As the forecasters begin the process of writing their scenarios
1. They must first describe the current language-teaching situation under consideration so that the picture which is revealed is accepted as valid by all those concerned, both in the institution and in the community.
2. They must design a model of the ideal language-teaching situation.
3. They must indicate the discrepancies between the current situation and the ideal.
4. They must make projections, forecasts and predictions regarding the future of language teaching based on their knowledge of the past and the present, and they must argue their way to consensus.
5. They must draw up three scenarios, the best, the worst and the most likely, showing in each case a possible but different sequence of events which may enhance or hinder efforts to move towards the ideal and/or probable end result.
At this point they can begin to consider what steps they and others can take to strengthen the possibility that the best rather than the worst scenario will be enacted, bearing in mind that change can occur through
– evolution or revolution
– leadership or drift
– negotiation or confrontation
– consensus or protest
– persuasion or dissuasion
– compromise or singlemindedness
and in a spirit of
– friendship or hostility
– honesty or dishonesty
¬ openness or deceit

A consideration of the future of language teaching requires a consideration of the future of education. One of the first books to be published that gave serious thought to the future was Alvin Toffler's *Future Shock* (1970). In it he remarked that 'people who must live in super-industrial societies will need new skills in three crucial areas: learning, relating and choosing'.[3] These three areas are applicable to language teaching:

1. *Learning – Students must learn how to learn.*

In these days of rapid change and complex international relations, the mastery of one additional language may not be sufficient. Students of the future will have to do more than absorb the specific grammatical items or generalizations of one language, they will need to grasp the strategies by which they can learn other languages.

2. *Relating – Education will have to teach students how to relate.*

There is a fear that the emphasis on science and technology will in time dehumanize people. Language teaching that is based on a humanistic communicative approach can bring people together in meaningful social interaction.

3. *Choosing – Education must systematically organize formal and informal activities that help students define, explicate and test their values.*

This can be done in language-teaching classrooms through a study of other cultures. By comparing and contrasting different customs, traditions, and mores students have an opportunity to develop their personal value systems by choosing among the alternatives.[4]

But what might teachers consider for themselves as they look ahead?

INVOLVEMENT

Teachers will have to play a more active part in shaping the future of language teaching. Language teachers cannot expect those who do not fully understand the nature and purpose of language teaching to make all the right decisions on their behalf without input from them. Through their professional organizations and in cooperation with community groups, teachers must influence the direction of language teaching or be prepared for the consequences.

UPGRADING

Teachers will have to keep abreast of the expanding pool of knowledge. These days knowledge is quickly outdated. Newly created knowledge will affect the direction that language teaching will take and the roles that language teachers will play. Unless teachers keep up-to-date through personal reading and retraining, they will be in no position to control their futures.

NEW ROLES

Teachers will have to create and adopt new roles. The traditional delivery systems for education are under attack. Education is facing an organizational revolution that will change the working conditions and roles of teachers and will incorporate new technology. New roles will be created for language teachers either with or without their cooperation.

Finally, what may be the future for communities?

THE COMMUNITY AS BENEFICIARY

Communities will have to expand their notions of the benefits that can accrue to them through second language teaching. In addition to providing political, economic and educational benefits, language teaching should be recognized as an important vehicle for bringing together people of divergent cultures through humanistic teaching. The greatest benefit communities could receive from language teaching would be a sense of cultural and linguistic harmony.

THE COMMUNITY AS RESOURCE

Communities will have to continue to give if they are to receive. Ultimately communities are responsible for the education of their members, young and old. The quantity and quality of the resources they supply to the teachers they hire will have a profound effect on the quantity and quality of education, including language teaching. Where human and material resources are not forthcoming, the returns will be slim.

THE COMMUNITY AS CONTROL

Communities will have to exercise responsible control over language teaching in cooperation with educators. The realm of education belongs solely to neither educators nor community members but is a shared responsibility. Good language programs result from a healthy partnership between the two groups.

There is an interesting cultural difference between native teachers of English and some non-native teachers of English which is clearly demonstrated when, in trying to elicit a particular verb form from their students, they use hand signals to point to the past, present or future. Native speakers of English usually point behind them for the past and in front of them for the future, suggesting perhaps that, individually and collectively, mankind has left behind a rapidly receding and forgotten past to step confidently forward into whatever lies ahead. Some non-native speakers of English, however, point in front of them for the past and behind them for the future, suggesting that the past is always in view and may be recalled, while mankind walks backwards into an unknown and uncertain future. Both cultural viewpoints are valid. The past is done but people can learn from it; the future may be unknown but not totally uncontrollable when knowledge, empathy, and cooperation prevail.

Activities

1. Preferably with the assistance of four or five other people, write the best, worst and most likely scenarios for a language program you are familiar with, following the steps outlined in this chapter.
2. From the eleven trends listed on pp. 133–5 pick three that might sometime in the future affect a language-teaching program in your community. Collect statistics and relevant information that will prove to others that if these trends materialize certain changes may have to be made to the program.

Afterthoughts

On the surface this book has been about second language teaching, but at a deeper level it has been about education in general. Communities around the world benefit from all sorts of different teaching activities. They supply resources to a wide range of subject-matter teachers. They exercise control over many kinds of educational institutions. Second language teachers are just one group among many groups who have a responsibility to think deeply and critically about current problems and practices in education. A wise and sensitive trilingual scholar said:

> Difficult and involved problems require the deep and continuing involvement of a community of truly committed scholars who focus coherent and meaningful effort on the totality of education and who stake their reputations and careers on the quality of the results. Problems that cut deeply into the reality of society, that affect vested interests, political interests, traditional prejudices – such problems imperatively require carefully safeguarded detachment and independence if their study is not to be a mockery of the search for truth. This is true for the study of political science, of sociology, of economics. It is even more true for the study of education.[1]

'No man is an island' wrote John Donne – and neither is a classroom. The sense of community which pervades any good classroom must spread to include those outside the classroom so that classroom and community, local and worldwide, can work together on common goals for the common good. Language makes it possible.

Appendix A Useful journals and newsletters for second language teachers

Applied Linguistics. Published three times a year by Oxford University Press: Walton Street, Oxford OX2 6DP, England, and 200 Madison Avenue, New York, NY 10016

Canadian Modern Language Review. Published four times a year: 237 Hellems Ave., Welland, Ontario L3B 3B8

English Around the World. A publication of the English-Speaking Union of the United States: 16 East 69th Street, New York, NY 10021

English Language Teaching Journal. Published four times a year by Oxford University Press: Walton Street, Oxford OX2 6DP, England, and 200 Madison Avenue, New York, NY 10016

English Teaching Forum. Published four times a year. Requests for subscriptions from teachers outside the United States should be addressed to the US Embassy in the capital city of the country in which the teacher resides. US residents should write to the Superintendent of Documents, US Government Printing Office, Washington DC

English Today. Published four times a year by Cambridge University Press: The Pitt Building, Trumpington Street, Cambridge CB2 1RP, England, and 32 East 57th Street, New York, NY 10022

Foreign Language Annals. American Council on Teaching Foreign Languages, Inc., 579 Broadway, Hastings-on-Hudson, NY 10706

IATEFL Newsletter. Published three times a year: IATEFL, 3 Kingsdown Chambers, Kingsdown Park, Whitstable, Kent CT5 2DJ, England

International Journal of the Sociology of Language. Published six times a year: Mouton Publishers, Walter de Gruyter, Inc., 200 Saw Mill River Road, Hawthorne, NY 10532

Journal of Reading – The Reading Teacher. Published by the International Reading Association. Membership in IRA includes a subscription to one of four journals: *The Journal of Reading* (secondary, college, adult), *The Reading Teacher* (elementary), *Reading Research Quarterly* (all levels), or *Lectura y Vida* (in Spanish): 800 Barksdale Road, P.O. Box 8139, Newark, Delaware, 19714

Language Learning. A journal of applied linguistics published four times a year: N4714 University Hospital, University of Michigan, Ann Arbor, Michigan, 48109

Language Problems and Language Planning. Journals Department, University of Texas Press, Box 7819, Austin, Texas, 78712

Reading in a Foreign Language. Published twice a year by the Modern Languages Department, University of Aston in Birmingham, England: Gosta Green, Birmingham, B47ET, England

TESL Canada Journal. Published twice a year. Membership in a provincial ESL association includes a subscription to the journal. TESL Canada Journal, Faculty of Education, McGill University, 3700 McTavish Street, Montreal, PQ H3A 1Y2

TESOL Newsletter. Published six times a year. Available only through membership in TESOL. TESOL, 202 DC Transit Building, Georgetown University, Washington, DC 20057

TESOL Quarterly. Membership in TESOL includes a subscription to the journal. TESOL, 202 DC Transit Building, Georgetown University, Washington, DC 20057

Appendix B   Language-teaching acronyms

EAL   English as an Additional Language
EAP   English for Academic Purposes
EFL   English as a Foreign Language
EIAL   English as an International Auxiliary Language
EIIL   English as an International/Intranational Language
EIL   English as an International Language
ELIC   English as a Language of International Communication
ELW   English as a Language of Wider Communication
ELT   English Language Teaching
EOP   English for Occupational Purposes
ESL   English as a Second Language
ESOD   English for Speakers of Other Dialects
ESOL   English for Speakers of Other Languages
ESP   English for Special/Specific Purposes
EST   English for Science and Technology
EWL   English as a World Language
FL   Foreign Languages
LFE   Local Forms of English
ML   Modern Languages
PRESL   Pre-school English as a Second Language
TEAL   Teachers of English as an Additional Language
TEFL   Teaching English as a Foreign Language
TESL   Teaching English as a Second Language
TESD   Teaching English as a Standard Dialect
TESOD   Teachers of English to Speakers of Other Dialects
TESOL   Teachers of English to Speakers of Other Languages
TTSE   Technological, Technical and Scientific English
TOEFL   Test of English as a Foreign Language

Appendix C International and national organizations

International organizations

Fédération Internationale des Professeurs de Langues Vivantes (FIPLV) – The
World Federation of Foreign Language Teachers Associations, D-355
Marburg/Lahnberge, West Germany
International Association of Teachers of English as a Foreign Language
(IATEFL), 3 Kingsdown Chambers, Kingsdown Park, Whitstable, Kent,
CT5 2DJ, England
International Bureau of Education, Palais Wilson, 1211 Geneva, Switzerland
International Council for Educational Development (ICED), 680 Fifth Avenue,
New York, NY 10019
International Institute for Educational Planning (IIEP), 7–9, rue Eugène Dela-
croix, F-75016, Paris, France
Teachers of English to Speakers of Other Languages (TESOL), 202 DC Transit
Building, Georgetown University, Washington, DC 20057
United Nations International Child Emergency Fund (UNICEF), United Nations,
New York, NY 10017·

National organizations

Within a nation, counties, states or provinces may have separate organizations.
Readers should therefore check to see what organizations exist in their region.

United States of America

Agency for International Development (AID), US Department of State, 320
21st Street, NW, Washington, DC 20523
Modern Language Association of America (MLA), 62 Fifth Avenue, New York,
NY 10011
National Association for Bilingual Education (NABE), 1201 16th Street, NW
Room 405, Washington, DC 20036
Peace Corps, Peace Corps Partnership Program (PCPP), 806 Connecticut
Avenue, NW Washington, DC 20525
Teachers of English to Speakers of Other Languages (TESOL), 202 DC Transit
Building, Georgetown University, Washington, DC 20057

Appendix C

Great Britain

British Council, 65 Davies Street, London, W1Y 2AA
Centre for Information on Language Teaching (CILT), 20 Carlton House Terrace, London SW1 5AP
English Speaking Union of the Commonwealth (ESU), 37 Charles Street, Berkeley Square, London W1X 8AB
Volunteer Service Overseas, 9 Belgrave Square, London SW1

Canada

Canadian Association of Second Language Teachers Inc. L'Association Canadienne des professeurs de langues secondes inc., 329 Overdale Street, Winnipeg, Manitoba, R3J 2G4
Canadian International Development Agency (CIDA), 122 Bank Street, Ottawa, Ontario, K1A 0G4
Canadian University Service Overseas (CUSO), 151 Slater Street, Ottawa, Ontario, K1P 5H5
TESL Canada. As the presidency moves from province to province, contact your provincial ESL association for the current address of TESL Canada.
World University Service of Canada, P.O. Box 3000, Station C, Ottawa, Ontario, K1Y 4M8

Australia

Australian Association for the Teaching of English, 163A Greenhill Road, Parkside, South Australia 5063
Australian Federation of Modern Language Teachers Associations, 112 Surrey Street, Darlinghurst, New South Wales 2010
Australian Volunteers Abroad, 262 Pitt Street, Sydney, New South Wales, 2000
English Speaking Union, 172 North Tee, Adelaide, South Australia 5000
Royal Overseas League, 365a Edgecliffe Road, New South Wales 2027

Notes

1 The community as beneficiary

1. Michael H. Long, 'Does second language instruction make a difference? A review of research', *TESOL Quarterly*, 17, 3 (September 1983), p. 359.
2. L. G. Kelly, *25 Centuries of Language Teaching: 500 B.C.–1969* (Rowley, Mass.: Newbury House, 1969), p. 396.
3. Report of the Unesco Meeting of Specialists, 1951, 'The use of vernacular languages in education' in Joshua A. Fishman, *Readings in the Sociology of Language* (The Hague: Mouton, 1968), pp. 689–90.
4. William A. Stewart, 'A sociolinguistic typology for describing national multilingualism' in Fishman, *Readings in the Sociology of Language*, pp. 540–1.
5. William F. Mackey, 'The description of bilingualism', *The Canadian Journal of Linguistics*, 7:2 (1962), pp. 58–9.
6. Edgar Faure et al., *Learning To Be* (Paris: Unesco, 1972), p. xxix.
7. Isaura Santiago Santiago, 'Third world vernacular/bi-multilingual curricula issues' in Beverly Hartford and Albert Valdman, eds. *Issues in International Bilingual Education: The Role of the Vernacular* (New York: Plenum Press), 1982, p. 126.
8. Charles A. Ferguson et al., 'Bilingual education – an international perspective' in Bernard Spolsky and Robert L. Cooper, eds., *Frontiers of Bilingual Education*, (Rowley, Mass.: Newbury House, 1977), p. 163.
9. Ibid., pp. 163–72.
10. Nancy Faires Conklin and Margaret A. Lourie, *A Host of Tongues* (New York: Collier Macmillan, 1983), p. 230.
11. E. Glyn Lewis, *Bilingualism and Bilingual Education* (Oxford: Pergamon Press, 1981), p. 322.
12. Conklin and Lourie, *A Host of Tongues*, p. 231.
13. Joshua A. Fishman, Robert L. Cooper and Andrew W. Conrad, eds. *The Spread of English* (Rowley, Mass.: Newbury House, 1977), pp. 6–34.
14. Quoted in Glyn Lewis, 'Implementation of language planning in the Soviet Union' in Juan Cobarrubias and Joshua A. Fishman, *Progress in Language Planning: International Perspectives* (New York: Mouton, 1983), p. 313.
15. Juan Cobarrubias, 'Ethical issues in status planning' in Cobarrubias and Fishman, *Progress in Language Planning*, p. 71.
16. Carol M. Eastman, *Language Planning: An Introduction* (San Francisco: Chandler and Sharp, 1983), pp. 164–5.

17. Joan Rubin, 'Bilingual education and language planning' in Spolsky and Cooper, *Frontiers of Bilingual Education*, pp. 284–5.
18. Lewis, *Bilingualism and Bilingual Education*, p. 262.
19. Joshua A. Fishman, 'Bilingual education: what and why?' in Margaret A. Lourie and Nancy Faires Conklin, eds., *A Pluralistic Nation: The Language Issue in the United States* (Rowley, Mass.: Newbury House, 1976), p. 409.
20. James Cummins, 'The construct of language proficiency in bilingual education' in James E. Alatis, ed., *Current Issues in Bilingual Education* (Washington, D.C.: Georgetown University Press, 1980), p. 97.

2 The community as resource

1. John Kenneth Galbraith, *The Anatomy of Power* (Boston: Houghton Mifflin, 1983), p. 14.
2. Ibid., p. 24.

3 The community as control

1. See the recent work of Basil Bernstein and Joan Tough.
2. R. Rosenthal and L. Jacobson, *Pygmalion in the Classroom: teacher expectations and pupils' intellectual development* (New York: Holt, Rinehart, Winston, 1968).
3. Carl A. Grant, *Community Participation in Education* (London: Allyn and Bacon, 1979). p. viii.
4. Michael Novak, *The Rise of the Unmeltable Ethnics* (New York: Macmillan, 1971), pp. 47–8.
5. John Friesen, *Schools With a Purpose* (Calgary: Detselig Enterprises, 1983), pp. 41–133.
6. James E. Allen, Jr, quoted in Grant, *Community Participation in Education*, p. 27.
7. John Martin Rich, *New Directions in Educational Policy* (Lincoln, Neb.: Professional Educators Publications, 1974), p. 54.
8. Alexander Israel Wittenberg, *The Prime Imperatives: Priorities in Education* (Toronto: Clarke Irwin, 1968), p. 72.
9. Jack C. Richards and Ted Rodgers, 'Method: Approach, Design and Procedure', *TESOL Quarterly*, 16, 2, June, 1982, pp. 153–64.
10. Robert Conry. Personal communication to the author.

4 National policies and language teaching

1. EPIE (Educational Products Information Exchange) Institute, *Instructional Materials Design Analysis*, (Berkeley, Ca.: EPIE Institute, 1977).
2. M. McDougal, H. Laswell and L. Chen, 'Freedom from discrimination in choice of language and international rights', *Southern Illinois University Law Journal*, 1 (1976), pp. 151–3.

3. Ibid., pp. 163–7.
4. Lau vs. Nichols, 414 US 563, 566 (1974).
5. Heinz Kloss, 'Language rights of immigrant groups', *International Migration Review*, 5 (1971), pp. 254–8.
6. John W. Meyer and Michael T. Hannon, *National Development and the World System: Educational, Economic and Political Change, 1950–1970* (Chicago: The University of Chigaco Press, 1979), pp. 37–8.
7. Ibid., p. 38.
8. Ibid., p. 52.
9. John Naisbitt, *Megatrends: Ten New Directions Transforming Our Lives* (New York: Warner Books, 1982), p. 7.
10. John Nisbet and Particia Broadfoot, *The Impact of Research on Policy and Practice in Education* (Aberdeen: Aberdeen University Press, 1980), p. 50.

5 Teaching English internationally

1. Andrew W. Conrad and Joshua A. Fishman, 'English as a world language: the evidence' in Joshua A. Fishman, Robert L. Cooper and Andrew W. Conrad, eds., *The Spread of English* (Rowley, Mass.: Newbury House, 1977), p. 6.
2. Joshua A. Fishman, Robert L. Cooper and Yehudit Rosenbaum, 'English around the world' in Fishman et al., *The Spread of English*, pp. 77–82.
3. Ibid., p. 105.
4. Ibid., p. 106.
5. Peter Strevens, *Teaching English as an International Language* (Oxford: Pergamon Press, 1980), p. 61.
6. H. G. Widdowson, 'English as an international language II: What do we mean by "International Language"?' in C. J. Brumfit, ed., *English for International Communication* (Oxford: Pergamon Press, 1982), p. 11.
7. Ibid., pp. 11–12.
8. Larry E. Smith, ed. *English for Cross-Cultural Communication* (London: Macmillan, 1981), p. xvii.
9. Robert L. Cooper and Fern Seckbach, 'Economic incentives for the learning of a language of wider communication: a case study' in Fishman et al., *The Spread of English*, p. 219.
10. Willard D. Shaw, 'Asian student attitudes towards English' in Smith, *English For Cross-Cultural Communication*, pp. 110–12.
11. Joshua A. Fishman, 'English in the context of international societal bilingualism' in Fishman et al., *The Spread of English*, p. 330.
12. David Lee Jackson, 'Ethics, politics, and foreign language teaching', unpublished paper, University of British Columbia, March, 1983, p. 1.
13. Ibid., p. 1.
14. Gloria Paulik Sampson, 'Exporting language teaching methods from Canada to China', *TESL Canada Journal*, 1, 1, January, 1984, p. 20.
15. Ibid., pp. 20–9.

6 Predicting the future in language teaching

1. John Naisbitt, *Megatrends*: *Ten New Directions Transforming Our Lives* (New York: Warner Books, 1982), p. 3.
2. Ibid., p. xxxii.
3. Alvin Toffler, *Future Shock* (New York: Bantam Books, 1970), p. 414.
4. Ibid., pp. 414–18.

Afterthoughts

1. Alexander Israel Wittenberg, *The Prime Imperatives* (Toronto: Clarke, Irwin, 1968), p. 44.

Bibliography

Alatis, James E. ed. *International dimensions of bilingual education*. Washington, DC: Georgetown University Press, 1978

Alatis, James E. ed. *Current issues in bilingual education*. Washington, DC: Georgetown University Press, 1980

Appleton, Nicholas. *Cultural pluralism in education: theoretical foundations*. New York: Longmans, 1983

Bailey, Richard and Manfred Gorlach, eds. *English as a world language*. Ann Arbor: University of Michigan Press, 1982

Brumfit, C. J. ed. *English for international communication*. Oxford: Pergamon Press, 1982

Buckingham, Thomas. *Needs assessment in ESL*. Washington, DC: Center for Applied Linguistics, 1981

Cobarrubias, Juan and Joshua A. Fishman, eds. *Progress in language planning: international perspectives*. New York: Mouton, 1983

Conklin, Nancy Faires and Margaret A. Lourie. *A host of tongues: language communities in the United States*. New York: Collier Macmillan, 1983

Conrad, Andrew W. and Joshua A. Fishman. 'English as a world language: the evidence' in Joshua A. Fishman et al., eds. *The spread of English*, Rowley: Mass.: Newbury House, 1977

Cooper, Robert L. and Fern Seckbach. 'Economic incentives for the learning of a language of wider communication: a case study' in Joshua A. Fishman et al., eds. *The spread of English*, Rowley, Mass.: Newbury House, 1977

Cummins, James. 'The construct of language proficiency in bilingual education' in James E. Alatis, ed. *Current issues in bilingual education*, Washington, DC: Georgetown University Press, 1980

Eastman, Carol M. *Language planning: an introduction*. San Francisco: Chandler and Sharp, 1983

Faure, Edgar et al. *Learning to be: the world of education today and tomorrow*. Paris: Unesco, 1972

Ferguson, Charles A. et al. 'Bilingual education – an international perspective' in Bernard Spolsky and Robert L. Cooper, eds. *Frontiers of bilingual education*. Rowley, Mass.: Newbury House, 1977

Ferguson, Marilyn. *The aquarian conspiracy: personal and social transformation in the 1980s*. Los Angeles: J. P. Tarcher, 1980

Fishman, Joshua A. *Language loyalty in the United States: the maintenance and perpetuation of non-English mother tongues by American ethnic and religious groups*. The Hague: Mouton, 1966

Bibliography

Fishman, Joshua A. ed. *Readings in the sociology of language*. The Hague: Mouton, 1968

Fishman, Joshua A. *Bilingual education: an international sociological perspective*. Rowley, Mass.: Newbury House, 1976

Fishman, Joshua A., Robert L. Cooper and Andrew W. Conrad, eds. *The spread of English: the sociology of English as an additional language*. Rowley, Mass.: Newbury House, 1977

Fishman, Joshua A., Charles A. Ferguson and Jyotirindra Das Gupta, eds. *Language problems of developing nations*. New York: Wiley, 1968

Galbraith, John Kenneth. *The anatomy of power*. Boston: Houghton Mifflin, 1983

Grant, Carl A. *Community participation in education*. London: Allyn and Bacon, 1979

Hartford, Beverly, Albert Valdman and Charles R. Foster, eds. *Issues in international bilingual education: the role of the vernacular*. New York: Plenum Press, 1982

Horvath, B. M. *The education of migrant children: a language planning perspective*. ERDC Report No. 24. Canberra: Australian Government Publishing Service, 1980

Jackson, David Lee. 'Ethics, politics, and foreign language teaching.' Unpublished paper, University of British Columbia, 1983

Kelly, L. G. *25 centuries of language teaching: 500 B.C. – 1969*. Rowley, Mass.: Newbury House, 1969

Kloss, Heinz. 'Language rights of immigrant groups', *International Migration Review*, 5, 1971

Lewis, E. Glyn. *Bilingualism and bilingual education*. Oxford: Pergamon Press, 1981

Long, Michael H. 'Does second language instruction make a difference? A review of research', *TESOL Quarterly*, 17, 3, September, 1983

Lourie, Margaret A. and Nancy Faires Conklin, eds. *A pluralistic nation: the language issue in the United States*. Rowley, Mass.: Newbury House, 1976

McDougal, M., H. Laswell and L. Chen. 'Freedom from discrimination in choice of language and international rights', *Southern Illinois University Law Journal*, 1, 1976

Mackey, William F. 'The description of bilingualism', *The Canadian Journal of Linguistics*, 7:2, 1962

Meyer, John W. and Michael T. Hannon. *National development and the world system: educational, economic and political change, 1950–1970*. Chicago: the University of Chicago Press, 1979

Naisbitt, John. *Megatrends: ten new directions transforming our lives*. New York: Warner Books, 1982

Nisbet, John and Patricia Broadfoot. *The impact of research on policy and practice in education*. Aberdeen: Aberdeen University Press, 1980

Novak, Michael. *The rise of the unmeltable ethnics*. New York: Macmillan, 1971

Report of the Unesco Meeting of Specialists, 1951. 'The use of vernacular languages in education' in Joshua A. Fishman, ed. *Readings in the sociology of language*. The Hague: Mouton, 1968

Rich, John Martin. *New directions in educational policy*. Lincoln, Neb.: Professional Educators Publications, 1974

Richards, Jack C. and Ted Rodgers. 'Method: approach, design and procedure', *TESOL Quarterly*, 16, 2, June, 1982

Rosenthal, R. and L. Jacobson. *Pygmalion in the classroom: teacher expectations and pupils' intellectual development*. New York: Holt, Rinehart, Winston, 1968

Rubin, Joan. 'Bilingual education and language planning' in Bernard Spolsky and Robert L. Cooper, *Frontiers of bilingual education*, Rowley, Mass.: Newbury House, 1977

Rubin, Joan and Bjorn H. Jernudd, eds. *Can language be planned? Sociolinguistic theory and practice for developing nations*. Honolulu: University Press of Hawaii, 1971

St. Clair, Robert, Guadalupe Valdes and Jacob Ornstein-Galicia. *Social and educational issues in bilingualism and biculturalism*. Washington, DC: University Press of America, 1981

Sampson, Gloria Paulik. 'Exporting language teaching methods from Canada to China', *TESL Canada Journal*, 1, 1, January, 1984

Santiago, Isaura Santiago. 'Third world vernacular/bi-multilingual curricula issues' in Beverly Hartford and Albert Valdman, eds. *Issues in international bilingual education*. New York: Plenum Press, 1982

Shaw, Willard D. 'Asian student attitudes towards English' in Larry E. Smith, *English for cross-cultural communication*, London: Macmillan, 1981

Smith, Larry E. ed. *English for cross-cultural communication*. London: Macmillan, 1981

Spolsky, Bernard and Robert L. Cooper. *Frontiers of bilingual education*. Rowley, Mass.: Newbury House, 1977

Stewart, William A. 'A sociolinguistic typology for describing national multilingualism' in Joshua A. Fishman, ed. *Readings in the sociology of language*. The Hague: Mouton, 1968

Strevens, Peter. *New orientations in the teaching of English*. Oxford: Oxford University Press, 1977

Strevens, Peter. *Teaching English as an international language: from practice to principle*. Oxford: Pergamon Press, 1980

Toffler, Alvin. *Future shock*. New York: Bantam Books, 1970

Wardhaugh, Ronald. *Language and nationhood: the Canadian experience*. Vancouver: New Star Books, 1983

Widdowson, H. G. 'English as an international language II: 'What do we mean by "International Language"?' in C. J. Brumfit, ed. *English for international communication*, Oxford: Pergamon Press, 1982

Wittenberg, Alexander Israel. *The prime imperatives: priorities in education*. Toronto: Clarke Irwin, 1968

Index of authors

Index of subjects

Africa 6–7, 13, 89, 115, 119
Amish 63
Argentina 90
Asia 6, 86, 89, 115, 119
Australia 17, 86–7, 99, 119, 124, 125

Belgium 6, 17
bilingual education 14–16, 17, 27–8, 61
Bilingual Education Act 16
Brazil 116
British Council 20, 125

CIDA (Canadian International Development Agency) 20
CUSO (Canadian University Service Overseas) 20, 125
Canada 6, 8, 12, 15, 17, 20, 63, 119, 122–4, 125
Chile 90
China 11, 13, 19, 88, 116, 122–4
citizenship 9, 21, 26, 30, 90, 92
colleagues 44–6, 76, 105
committees 48, 55, 75, 104, 108
communities
  assessing 38
  benefits to 3–30, 37, 84, 137
  common interest 33–5, 51, 56–64
  control by 50–84, 137
  decision making 37, 55, 64
  geo-political 7, 33, 39–40, 51
  participation 55
  professional 34, 51, 64–8
  publications 48–9
  resources 29, 32–49, 56, 137
  services 48–9
  speech 7, 33, 58–9

computers 65, 96
Cuba 58, 90
cultural maintenance 14, 22–4, 30, 36, 59–60, 100
cultural pluralism 8, 22, 24, 48, 60, 94, 95, 134
culture 9, 14, 15, 21, 30, 48
curriculum 14, 22, 28, 45, 48, 54, 64, 71–2, 79, 82
Czechoslovakia 90

developing nations 3, 6, 11, 19, 36, 87, 115, 124, 133

EPIE (Educational Products Information Exchange) 95
East Germany 90
economic development 10–11, 23, 24, 36
economic security 3, 10, 14, 15, 23, 59, 86–7, 134
elected educational authorities 54–6
employment 9, 21, 40, 97, 100–2
English
  EFL 11, 19–20, 117
  ESL 16–17, 21, 89, 117
  ESP 20–1, 131
  dialects 18, 58
  local forms 119–20
  spread 114–16, 133
  users 116–17
  uses 117–19
ethics 20, 120–2
ethnic groups see minority groups
Europe 7, 65, 86–7, 98, 114

families 33, 35, 56–8